To my friend,
Richard

Arline Witte

PASSION,

POWER

&

PROPHECY

Human life

is the infancy of our

immortality.

A. E. WITTE

PASSION, POWER

and

PROPHECY

by

A. E. Witte

📖 STATUS PUBLISHERS, INC. 📖

Connecticut

PASSION, POWER AND PROPHECY

Hardcover Trade Edition

ISBN 1-888122-00-5

LCCN 95-25582

CIP DATA may be found on Page 220.

Published by STATUS PUBLISHERS, Cheshire, CT 06410-0892

Printed and manufactured in the U.S.A.

TABLE OF CONTENTS

It happened suddenly, like an

explosive flash of summer lightning,

full of fire and drama.

The pretty woman has no warning that something is about to happen. Her perfume leaves a soft trail in the air as she enters her living room and her blue silk robe moves gracefully around smooth, shapely legs. Suddenly, she senses someone calling to her from far away — a man's voice — rich, resonant and decidedly British. Its distinctive sound shatters her calm and drifts into her mind, touching the core of her existence.

"Elizabeth . . ."

She turns in the direction of the voice so quickly that long strands of her soft honey-blonde hair are caught between her slightly-parted pink lips. The television screen has somehow jumped to life, revealing the master of the voice — a distinctive man she has never seen before in this lifetime — an actor, costumed from the pages of history. As he speaks, his words are a blur, but something strange is happening. Forbidden memories, fallen through the cracks of time, are struggling to emerge. *Something is awakening . . .*

A chill climbs into her flesh with icy fingers.

Her heartbeat races and roars in her ears. Her throat closes shut. She gasps for a breath. A wave of sorrow whips her trembling body as her searching eyes explore his singular masculinity and the sensuous way he moves. Each gesture is like a secret ceremony, a velvet touch that probes every inch of her body, mind and soul. Just like a time-capsule buried in the long-ago past, bittersweet memories spring to her mind as his face appears before her, larger than life, transparent, floating in mid-air. But she's not afraid. He's gazing at her with adoration.

His powerful presence challenges her, compelling her recognition. Suddenly, five unspoken words gently force their message into her consciousness and penetrate her fiercely throbbing heart.

"Remember me, Elizabeth. Remember me."

Instant recognition wraps around her like a comforting mist and she draws in the deepest breath of her life, then releases it in a prolonged sigh. Her crystal-blue eyes grow moist as she watches his virile dignity through the contour of long, dark eyelashes, savoring him as one would enjoy a rare vintage wine. She studies him tenderly as he wanders across an elegant theatrical set, proud and regal, with a tall man's long stride. Memories spread like wildfire. She begins to remember him *the way he was then*. His hair is still sleek, dark as night without stars. She savors those intelligent eyes, eyes the color of brandy when warmed by candlelight.

She knows him from another time, another place.

Time cannot erase such wonderful memories .... the finely-sculptured profile she used to trace with her delicate fingers .... his coiled power and daring courage . . . those huge expressive hands, moving and gesturing so dramatically.

His mouth reveals images only she can understand. Her heart races so fast, she believes she's going to die. She starts to speak to the ghostly image before her, but without warning, the television screen goes blank again. *He's gone.*

A sudden weakness clutches her in an unwelcome embrace and she allows her arms to relax by her sides. Neatly-polished fingertips loosen their grip on the file of documents she has been holding all this time, spilling its contents toward the floor. Bright islands of white paper drift to the carpet and settle at her sandaled feet. Hypnotically, she stares down at them, still dazed by the stranger who has stepped out from the shadows of eternity.

But he isn't a stranger.

And her name isn't Elizabeth.

Through a stormy veil of tears, she finds the sofa and collapses into its soft pillows, yielding to the shattering sense of loss she feels. The man has completely transformed her life in sixty seconds. But she feels reborn. Something wonderful, something terrifying, has just happened here.

She wants to know what. She needs to know why.

That's how it all began . . .

What you're about to read is based on actual events.

This is a startling tale, a twilight blend of mysterious images, secret memories and bizarre happenings written under a cloak of secrecy.

Until now . . .

It's here, in our present time, that you'll find the results of the distant past and its dangerous adventures, courage of heroic proportions and the exposé of seductive mysteries.

You'll also find awesome inner powers which have laid dormant in suffering humanity for untold ages. And you'll discover poignant, timeless passions which have outlasted the dark centuries between *then* and *now*, like a flickering candle-flame in a midnight sky.

In the fascinating past, a well-known actor named Lance* journeyed to New York City to follow a dream.

He found his heart waiting for him — his other half, a delicate dancer named Elizabeth.*

Their bonding is the essence of myths and legends, living proof that lasting love can survive the mystical centuries, savage butchery, and resurface in a magical rebirth.

At the moment they met, their destinies were forever changed, forever fused . . . like gold, melting into itself.

He was the moth and she was the flame.

Or was it the other way around?

All names & certain personal facts have been changed in the interest of privacy.

It is for us that *the new Elizabeth* has been chosen to come forward at this most tragic and dramatic time in earth's history, to tell of the magic and the mystery — *some call them miracles* — she has endured. But the truest miracle of all is that she has survived. She takes a serious risk in revealing herself in these pages, but as she strips her soul bare and speaks the truth, she helps us to move toward a more fulfilling life through the fascinating portrait of another time, another place, showing us how easily the past fits into the present.

Through her words, so rich with unconditional love, a timely theme merges with an amazing journey into the unknown, giving us a gift that money can't buy. For your exclusive guided tour, there are no long airport lines, no crowds, no luggage to pack and no reservations to make. As the excitement unfolds, recline on a lush tropical beach, unwind in your favorite chair or curl up in bed as you move through time toward the ultimate ecstasy.

Like a voyager from another world, your true adventure will escort you into the fascinating past, then you'll fast-forward into our present time, where you'll discover the source of life and the best-kept secret of the ages. And you'll *know* how to develop your inner powers, *like her* . . . but with each day, savage secrets rape Elizabeth's life with the sudden force of a summer storm, full of jagged lightning, thunder and passion.

Out of this storm came a man.

And a love that was born nearly two centuries ago.

But to understand the bizarre events that are happening now, let's take a look into the past *to discover its beginnings.*

Step back with me, to another time, another place.

As we move silently into the past, we discover a forgotten world, New York City as it existed nearly two centuries ago, a civilized era when the pace of life was leisurely and unhurried, a romantic time when gallant gentlemen courted lovely ladies in the darkness of horse-drawn carriages.

Imagine a gracious season of splendor and gentility when serious crime seemed non-existent . . . a tender season glorified by tightly controlled passions, elegant manners and silver sleigh bells . . . when young girls in white dresses flirted cautiously behind dainty lace fans . . . when soft candlelight shimmered everywhere, cobblestone streets glowed under street lamps lit with flame, and lavish Victorian lace was the style of the day.

It was a time of maple-sugar candy and the scent of sandalwood, a time of pinafores and parasols . . . and peace.

A time when the world was young and full of hope.

A time of innocence and great destinies.

A time when love lasted forever.

In this tranquil era, Elizabeth's startling legend begins.

As fragile as the miniature sculptures she collects, it's only when she dances that she can escape the trapped feelings which torment her days and keep her awake at night.

Elizabeth has a delicate beauty. Her flawless skin is the color of rose-tinted cream and the blush on her cheeks is like sunset on snow. Blue-sapphire eyes gaze through a dark fringe of impossibly long eyelashes and a wreath of golden chestnut hair surrounds her face, hair so luxurious that it begs to be caressed. Starry shadows play in its silken waves, reflecting light even in darkness. Her body is feminine, with graceful legs made even more beautiful by scores of encore performances.

Smooth as sheer pink satin, Elizabeth's curvaceous body reveals an impatient virgin's silent message to a man she has yet to meet. *Love me*, it seems to whisper with its softly elegant movements, but her older brother has sent all of her handsome male admirers away. He withholds the love his younger sister needs and theirs is a strained relationship, full of conflict.

They were fortunate to find their current surroundings, a large studio with small lodging rooms in the rear, suitable for a brother and sister. Elizabeth's favorite place is the front studio, where she shares her love of music and dance with her eager young students while Ethan is at work.

On the antique dresser in her bedroom, a blue velvet purse lays open to our gaze, and we look inside. A lace-edged handkerchief, monogrammed with the letter *E*, gently touches a butter-soft leather change purse and a shiny silver latch-key nestles in neatly-folded blue gloves. Along the purse's blue interior, we find a tiny golden fan-shaped mirror, lip pomade, a petite vial of her favorite French perfume, and a diamond ring.

Near her purse, like a miniature shrine in a Victorian silver frame, is a tintype photograph of her adored father and mother, both deceased. This picture, and the diamond ring bequeathed to Elizabeth by her mother, are the only things that are truly hers. Her fingerprints are visible on the photograph's protective glass, revealing all the times she's held it, longing for their impossible return. Today, it bears the mark of tears.

As we move further into a world of two centuries ago, we find Elizabeth, alone. She's staring at her swan ballet costume, remembering her successes as a ballerina to push away her sadness, but the breakfast-time quarrel with her insensitive brother has tinted her cheeks a stormy shade of red and her face is wet with tears. Restless, she wanders to the windows and watches as winter's first snowfall drifts leisurely from a darkened violet sky.

Impulsively, she flings open the leaded-glass windows. Frozen air rushes in, soothing her reddened cheeks. She breathes deeply in a failed attempt to calm her shattered nerves, then reaches outside, catching snowflakes in her hands and pressing them against her cheeks.

A shiver darts through her flesh. Quickly, she shuts the windows against the howling wind and the latches close with a loud *click!* She sighs aloud as she slowly walks to her lonely bed, unbuttoning her dress with slender, graceful fingers. It flutters off her creamy shoulders and drifts to the floor, along with her ruffled white petticoat.

Elizabeth stands nearly nude, clad in lacy lingerie from Paris, her only extravagance in a life filled with dark shadows. A look of pleasure crosses her face as she lifts the costume over her head, slowly allowing it's silk lining to slide over her nearly-naked body. The look in her eyes reveals what she's feeling and as she closes her eyes, we can sense the depth of her passion flowing through her mind and into her flesh.

The thought makes her feel more alone than ever and her hands tremble as she slips her delicate feet into the slightly-worn ballet shoes, but it's more of an embrace as she curves their satin ribbons around her deer-slender ankles.

Gathering her hair in both hands, she draws it up in one quick movement, securing it tightly with decorative gold hairpins. She enjoys the feeling of carefully arranging each silky wave with ladylike precision, then she pulls just a few lustrous curls onto her forehead, her cheeks and the gently curved nape of her neck. Finally, she places the delicate swan-feathers around her face.

As they caress her cheeks with their sensuous softness, she glances in the mirror and a smile replaces the sadness of the morning.

The illusion is complete.

Elizabeth is ready to face her audience.

If only she could know. . .

Tonight, she will find what she's been looking for, in a way that she never expected.

Part 1

THE

FORBIDDEN

JOURNEY

Chapter 1:

SECRET CEREMONIES

(Elizabeth is speaking.)

When I look back, I realize that my life hadn't really begun until that night in December, when lacy snowflakes drifted to earth and the sky turned a passionate shade of violet. I unlocked the studio's front door for my ballet students and placed a discreet sign in the front windows to announce next week's performances. Just then, the storybook scene beyond the windows captured my attention.

Outside, a horse-drawn carriage quickened its pace. The horse's hooves clattered on the cobblestones with a spirited sound as silhouettes of men and women hurried past my windows, their capes billowing in the wind and covered with a fine layer of new snow. The old lamplighter walked with difficulty as he pressed his aged body against the gusting wind. He tipped his hat to me as he passed, and I waved to him. At the touch of his flaming rod, the light leaped brightly through the studio's leaded-glass window panes, forming patterns on the golden oak floor. Just then, the clock chimed. I quickly lit all the candles and hurried back to my room. After glancing in my mirror, I pressed extra face powder onto my reddened cheeks until they turned palest pink. Once again, I'll be able to keep my bitter relationship with Ethan a secret from the world.

Suddenly, the rising sound of enthusiastic student voices calling my name welcomed me back to reality.

I quickly ran into the dance studio.

My heart pounded with an untamed wildness, as it always did when I witnessed the scene before me, dancers preparing to dance. Like fine instruments in a symphony orchestra, eager young men and women stretched and warmed their perfected bodies. Then the sound of rustling costumes filled the studio as they gathered around me, smiling and talking until the music began for my opening number.

I ascended the stage and waited for my musical cue.

Finally, the moment came and I moved swiftly. My white costume glittered in the glow of candle-flame footlights and fragile swan wings floated and pursued me as I whirled and circled the stage. Sometimes, I *became* the music, and tonight, I've lost myself completely to its graceful flow.

But tonight, everything seemed different. A sudden wave of emotion swept through me, like a hot gust of wind before an approaching summer storm. A new intense sensation flowed through me and I was aware that something extraordinary had just happened. A dark stranger had entered the studio.

With each pirouette's turn, I caught fleeting glimpses of him. Tall and distinguished, nobility shone around him like a princely aura as he quietly shook the snow from his silk top-hat and black cape and placed them neatly on an empty chair near the front door.

When he turned toward the stage, a startled look crossed his face. He stood motionless for several minutes, then the man in black moved forward. Elegant and theatrical, the stranger came toward the stage with a controlled swiftness and tall man's long stride, nearer and nearer, parting the crowd as he moved, until he was close to the stage.

Under his intense gaze, a new emotion thrust itself through me, a rare depth I had never known before. Enchanted visions blurred my vision and I was ecstatic with the promises they made. A wondrous new creativity was suddenly using me, guiding my body and shaping my dance performance into an unexpected work of art. I found myself attempting daring new steps, faster pirouettes, higher leaps and surprising pauses, bringing alternate gasps and applause from my audience.

The man shouted, "Bravo! Bravo!" His voice echoed in my mind and found a home there, as I soared across the stage with the gossamer delicacy of winged feet. My body obeyed every command and rapture glowed brightly within me. My warming flesh revealed an imprisoned passion, and I grew hotter and hotter with each passing moment.

My emotions were at a fever-pitch as the last musical note sounded, and as my performance ended, I bowed in a deep curtsy to the applause of my wildly cheering audience. And when I raised my head with a smile, his eyes caught mine and wouldn't let go. I could see him clearly now.

He's the kind of man that women can only dream about.

He moved closer. Finally, we were an arm's-length apart.

His eyes were full of worship and the warmth behind his smile was as intimate as a forbidden touch.

His hair, dark as a midnight sky, made his skin look even whiter by comparison. He displayed a natural elegance and in his stance, I sensed a virile masculinity.

Without asking, he reached up with both arms to lift me down from the stage. I was irresistibly drawn to him and I leaned forward. His strong hands circled my waist and gently brought me down, close to him.

I could feel his breath on my face, he was so near.

His hands lingered on my waist moments longer than necessary, and his eyes blazed with sensual promise, an inner fire born of the yearning I could see in their depths.

They gazed deeply into mine and held me with a power as old as time itself. My cheeks blushed the color of a scarlet rose and my virgin passion stirred.

For an instant, my whole body trembled. He reacted with a long, audible breath, then removed his hands from my waist and spoke in a voice that flowed through me like golden honey.

His singular sound seemed to come from a mysterious place. It reached deep inside of him, and when it emerged, it had transformed itself into a celestial sound, rich and resonant, a velvet smoothness that warmed my flesh and soothed my soul.

And those eyes . . so dark and mysterious, so compelling, so intense, like a volcano just before it erupts.

We stood without moving for what seemed like a very long time, staring into each other's eyes. I felt as if I've known him before. *I've never been so moved by any other man.*

Everyone was silent, watching us. I called out to the musicians, "Please continue." The ballet rehearsal continued, and beautiful music filled the air as we moved toward two empty chairs. We spoke in hushed tones, and I recall only a few of the words which passed between us, only a fragment or two, but they are words I'll always remember.

"Now that I've finally found you, I cannot let you go." His voice left a soft trail in the air. Everything was happening so quickly. My breath came in heart-pounding waves and my costume felt unbearably tight. My lungs fought desperately for air. I felt faint and reached out to him. He put his arm around my shoulders to steady me.

"Are you all right? " I nodded *yes*. With his hand, he lifted my chin until our eyes met. "May I call you Elizabeth? " The gentle look he found in my eyes brought a smile to his face, then to mine.

"I apologize. I shouldn't have spoken so boldly. Can you forgive me? " When I nodded, he leaned close and whispered, "There must be a God, for who else could have gathered all the stars from the sky, just to put them in your beautiful eyes." His gaze lulled me, like a personal lullaby.

My body feels soft and warm.
I feel as if I'm floating . . .

I was barely aware of what he was saying, our gazes intertwined as they were. I did hear his name, though ... Lance. He's a well-known actor from England, newly arrived in New York on tour with a company of European stage performers. He's brought his sister along, too. Her name is Anne and she desperately yearns for a successful career on the stage.

"Destiny must have brought me here tonight, Elizabeth. I came to arrange private music and ballet lessons for my sister, but I hadn't known that tonight, I'd find the perfect woman, the one woman I've been searching for, *all of my life*." He took a deep breath, then released it in a long gasp as his eyes searched my face. "My God, Elizabeth, you *are* exquisite." He and I were locked in some kind of secret ceremony, an intense force more forceful than life itself. I was held tightly within his dynamic presence, unable to move, not wanting to . . . time was disappearing for me and I had the sense that reality was gone.

Minutes later, he glanced at his gold pocket-watch. "I must leave now. My performance begins soon, but before I go, promise that you'll let me take you to dinner at six tomorrow night. After dinner, if you wish, I can arrange for a front row seat at my performance. Please say you will." I smiled *yes*.

As he hurried out into the snowy night, his departing gaze excited me, exalted me.

Like an embrace, climbing into my soul for sanctuary.

Chapter 2:

SAND CASTLES & NIGHT WHISPERS

Weeks and months came and went swiftly, like a wisp of smoke in a strong breeze. Although cold and frosty, January grew warm in my consciousness and the winds of February could not chill me, for I was filled with an inner warmth. My days and nights overflowed with thoughts of Lance, swirling through my mind like finest silk.

Lance attended each evening performance of my ballet, attentively watching from his front-row seat while holding a huge bouquet of flowers in his lap.

In my profession, I had never danced for only one person before, but now, I danced for Lance alone.

At the end of every performance, he presented me with a lavish bouquet. As I'd bow low to accept it, our eyes would always meet in a lightning blaze of rising adoration as his lips formed the silent words, *I love you.* Suddenly, I no longer heard the thunderous applause of my audience. All I could hear was Lance's unspoken words of love. And at his performances as *Hamlet*, my love showed shamelessly in my applause.

He had become the brightest star in my universe.

Whether onstage or off, Lance's stance emphasized his masculine form and his face portrayed an elegant gauntness. His nose had been broken in a childhood accident, but he was good-natured about the permanent dent it made on the bridge of his nose. He laughed as he showed me his profile.

"Gives me added character, don't you think? "

Even so, Lance had a lord-of-the-manor presence and I could easily imagine a medieval stone castle or gothic mansion somewhere in his brooding past or his artistic present, lavishly decorated with heraldic symbols, a knight's antique armor, with family crests and rich tapestries proudly displayed along stately castle walls, proper surroundings for such a regal man.

Lance was born to play *Hamlet*.

At the end of each performance, he brought his audience to their knees, then to their feet, wanting more, needing more. Each time I'd watch my noble British actor perform, my heart would beat in rhythm to the commanding pulse of his words.

And each evening, he stole my heart like a gentle pirate.

It was difficult for me to keep my passions under control, but I knew that I must, for a man in our time highly valued a virgin bride. Although Lance never demanded more than an innocent kiss from me, I could sense that his control was as unyielding as mine. Still, his virile masculinity was powerfully seductive. Every fleeting gesture and each word he spoke delivered an enticing message straight to my heart.

Surely, this was a descent from Mount Olympus.

Winter's chill had finally turned its face toward the sun, yielding to April's springtime rebirth. May brought colorful wildflowers, leafy foliage, and Sunday picnics in the park by a blue-mirror lake, where we'd watch white swans glide leisurely across its surface. But sometimes, Lance and I would take horse-drawn surrey rides into the countryside, or leisurely stroll along tree-lined pathways, alone in our private world of two. One Sunday, he told me about his happy childhood in England and I could hear the sweet nostalgia in his voice.

Time passed swiftly for us. Soon, early summer gifted us with sparkling days and brilliant yellow sunshine. But June's warm breezes turned hot as fire in July. Often, we'd travel to the seashore to escape the city's heat and laughed as we built elaborate fantasy castles in the cool, wet sand. Our sand castle seemed perfect to me, but Lance, so eager to please, added towers, turrets, and a water-filled moat!

How we adored the feeling of cool sea breezes blowing through our hair as we watched lively blue-green waves lap at the shore. We escaped our worries in the simple pleasures of children, entertaining each other with fantastic stories of the people who might have lived in such castles. We shared our enchanted visions and medieval scenes of opulent banquets, of gallant knights defending fair maidens, of great halls where kings roamed and held court, of beautiful young women in exquisite ball gowns dancing with handsome young men. I could easily imagine Lance in such noble surroundings.

Later, the setting sun cast a coral glow over our make-believe kingdom, and although the setting sun was beautiful to see, I was always sad. Our fairyland sand castle would soon disappear, washed away by the rising tide.

By tomorrow, our dream castle would be only a memory.

We would sit close in the darkness of the horse-drawn surrey, enjoying the moonlit countryside as we traveled back to the city on those quiet summer evenings.

Lance's voice was barely perceptible over the clatter of horse's hooves as he whispered his love for me. I anticipated our future with secret thoughts, well-hidden until our eyes met. Again and again we were tested as our passions would rise within us. Like a windstorm, they threatened to engulf us with their unbearable intensity if they were not restrained.

Lance's controlled power served us both well.

One sunny Sunday, we planned a picnic in the park, and now, Lance was spreading a soft quilt in the shade of the stately oak. Feathery-white clouds floated in a blissful blue sky and a strong breeze fluttered through my hair, billowing curls across my face. Lance gently lifted each curl from my face.

"I feel as if I'm unveiling a fragile statue. You're so delicate, I'm afraid you'll break." Strolling couples stared at us and I blushed pink in my embarrassment.

"Let them look," Lance grinned.

After we had consumed our delicious picnic feast, we rested in the shade of our special oak while Lance read aloud from my favorite book of poetry. I gazed at him with my full attention, but I listened with my heart alone. He spoke with a commanding, pulsing rhythm, and I could see the passion move across his face as his voice became more intimate. I was barely aware of his words. His eyes and the sensual curve of his mouth held my attention. How I adored his manly ways and the infinite depths I could see deep in his eyes.

The love I saw there seemed to pull me in.

I would willingly drown in such a blissful lake.

When he finished reading, he stood quickly. His form was silhouetted against the sun and he appeared so tall that he could touch the sky if he wanted to. And if he reached even further, he could steal fire from the sun.

Perhaps I'll ask him for a star.

He looked down at me and smiled, then he kissed my hand. "Stay here while I gather wildflowers for your hair."

I watched his manly stride as he walked away from me. He had awakened such profound longings in me — yearnings so strange, so wonderful and so frightening.

Suddenly, summer's gentle breeze billowed into a gust of wind, whipping Lance's dark hair in the sunlight. Deep down inside of me, I felt an agony that was more like ecstasy, a throbbing ache that filled me with its longing and its ravenous hunger, a power screaming for release.

Stirred by my passion, I opened my book of poetry, and inside, I wrote the words that were swirling through my mind.

"My beloved: In the enchanted forest of the night, you reign supreme, my only love. A sorcerer's magic is at your mind's command. Oh magician, hypnotize my will, exorcise my pain, release my imprisoned passion and bring me home to the stars. When our eyes meet, sweet fantasies upon Camelot snow we doth commit. I watch, spellbound, as heavenly forces genuflect to your perfection. You are Merlin. I am Circé. Together, we are love itself."

I held the book on my lap, patiently waiting for Lance's return. Minutes later, he came back to me with flowers for my hair. With a mysterious smile, I handed the book to him, open to his tribute. His look of surprise turned into a smile as he read, his form silhouetted against the sun. Then his smile disappeared and was replaced by a more intense emotion. His chest rose and fell with the profound depth of his breathing. He never raised his eyes from the page and he ignored the sweat, running down his face like little rivers, as his passion took command of him. He read my tribute five or six times.

Then he reached down, circled my waist with one arm and lifted me up to him with a muscular strength he had never shown to me before. My lips were moist and waiting as he pulled my trembling body close to his. I could feel his passion rising as he pulled me tight up against himself.

Deep inside of me, I could feel the same desperate hunger he was trying to control in himself. Suddenly, he put his hands around my waist and gently moved me away from him, his head bowed, his body leaning forward. "Oh, my God . . . forgive me, Elizabeth," he gasped. His face spoke of torment, a new anguish I'd never seen before. Then he turned away from me and I could see him breathing deeply, slightly bent over, his hands on his knees, his head bowed. Endless minutes passed. Finally, he stood upright. His shoulders rose and fell as he drew in a deep breath, then released it.

At last, he turned to face me again.

"Will you marry me, beautiful lady? "

I whispered a breathless, "*Oh yes*," and happiness shone in his eyes as he continued to speak. His words like lightning, they came so fast! "I will not return to England. Except for my sister Anne, the rest of my family is deceased. I'll contact my estate agent tomorrow and sell my property in England and I'll marry you and stay here with you forever, my sweet angel." He paused for a moment, then leaned close and held my small hands in his. His voice was rich and his eyes moist as he whispered words I'll remember till the universe dissolves.

"You have become my life, Elizabeth. My very breath."

My heart was so full I could barely speak and my tears fell onto my white dress. Lance took his handkerchief from his pocket and dried my tears. Within minutes, his sense of humor made me smile. The tears were gone and would not return.

"Will next month — August — give you enough time to prepare? " I nodded *yes*, and we spent the rest of the afternoon by the lake of blue mirror, laughing and making wedding plans while white swans glided by.

I can't wait to tell my brother.

"For God's sake, Elizabeth, he's an actor!"

Ethan's face reddened with anger as he shouted at me, loud and long. "He'll break your heart, then he'll throw you away!" He turned his face and slumped into his chair by the fireplace. He stared into winter's dead ashes and muttered, "I thought you'd be over this schoolgirl crush by now. Besides, he's too old for you!"

"Lance is only ten years older than I am." I turned, trying to leave the room and this argument, but he continued to shout.

"Mark my words, my foolish sister. He'll take you and use you, if he hasn't already!" He bolted out of his chair, grabbed my shoulders and shook me hard.

"Has he? If he's stolen your virginity, I'll kill him!"

"No! Lance never touched me in that way!"

"Damn it, Lizzie, tell me the truth!" Ethan's painful grip tightened around my shoulders. I cried, but he wouldn't stop.

"That IS the truth, *and don't call me Lizzie!* Now let me go!" But my words made him more furious. The anger in his eyes frightened me as much as his voice as he shouted at me, mere inches in front of my pale trembling face.

"I'll let you go when you tell me the truth! Are you still a virgin? " He kept pushing me backwards, toward the sofa.

"Yes, of course I'm still a virgin! Now let me go . . . *please, Ethan.*"

But my brother was enjoying his latest mastery over me. He squeezed me tighter and kept shoving me.

I cried out, "You're hurting me!" I twisted my body and pulled myself out of his grasp. "Don't ever hurt me again, Ethan! When I'm married, you'll never again be able to . . ."

He raised his finger and pointed it at me like a gun, and when he spoke, his voice was rigid as steel and twice as cold.

"This wedding of yours will never happen. *I forbid you to marry him.* Chapel bells will never ring for you and that actor, you little fool!"

"I won't let you drive Lance away, just as you've driven all my other suitors away. Not this time."

Ethan's face grew redder and the veins on his temples bulged with each word. "You'll do as I say, *Lizzie.* You will not marry *until I say you can.* And you will only marry someone of my choosing, a man of substance, someone rich and powerful."

He stared hard at me and ran his finger lightly down my cheek. "You're beautiful. Your mirror will tell you the truth of it. Because of your beauty, you can have any man you want, with my permission." He shook his head.

"But I cannot understand why you want to marry that — I find it hard to even say the word — actor!"

"For a reason you couldn't possibly understand, Ethan. I love him. I'll never marry a man I don't love, even if you try to force me into it. You should know me well enough by now!"

"And you know *me* well enough, *Lizzie*, to realize that I'll *never* let you marry that actor. In a few months, he'll be going back to England and you'll forget all about him."

I stood in front of him, shaking my head *no,* but at that moment, my blood ran cold. Ethan's hands turned into fists.

"Maybe I should have a little talk with your actor friend. But first, I think you need some talking to, *Lizzie . . .*"

He came toward me with anger flaming his hard eyes like visible flames. *I've never seen him this angry before.*

I screamed and turned to run to my bedroom, where I'd be safe behind my locked door, but as I ran out of the parlor, tears clouded my vision and I tripped over the curio case where I kept my small sculptures.

My precious collection of memories crashed to the floor.

Porcelain cherubs, winged angels, carousel horses, tiny unicorns, and the pearly seashells Lance and I had gathered at the seashore on all those lovely summer days . . . miniatures of all the things I love so much . . .

Destroyed.

Now they were only a mound of powdery glitter.

I fell to my knees and wept as Ethan cursed and stormed out into the hot summer night.

Chapter 3:

FROM THIS DAY FORWARD

A few weeks have passed since that unhappy night, but now, my wedding day has finally arrived. August has given us a special wedding present, an unusually cool spell of weather accompanied by a golden August morning.

Ever since the engagement, Ethan's resentment had hung in the air like an approaching thunderstorm, and Lance worried about Ethan's uncontrollable rage.

"Elizabeth, I have to do something before this escalates into a dangerous situation. I'm afraid he'll hurt you."

And so, last night, Lance escorted me home after his final performance. As we entered the parlor, Ethan looked up from his newspaper, then went back to his reading, ignoring us both. Lance stepped forward and spoke.

"You and I have important things to discuss, Ethan."

"There's nothing to say. Get out of my house!"

Lance stood firm. "Do you love your sister? "

"That's a foolish question. Of course I do!"

"Then why do you put her through this torture? "

"What torture? I don't know what you're talking about!"

Ethan folded his newspaper on his lap and tried hard to look relaxed, but sweat poured down his face from under his sideburns and he squirmed in his chair as Lance continued.

"You're trying to ruin the happiest time of Elizabeth's life. When you cancelled the flowers, that was easy to fix. But you've done many other things that hurt her. The worst thing you've done was to tell the minister that I've bewitched her, and that he must stop this wedding in the name of God. Didn't you realize that he'd speak to her about it? "

"I did no such thing," Ethan shrugged.

"Are you calling the minister a liar? "

"Get out, Maycroft! I have nothing more to say to you."

"But I have something more to say to you. Mark my words, I *will* marry Elizabeth tomorrow. You won't be able to stop the wedding, no matter what you do. If only you knew how much I adore her. I would die for her."

"You may have to."

"Is that a threat? "

"Take it as you will," Ethan replied coldly.

Lance ignored the danger. "Elizabeth told me that you want her to marry an important man, a man with money. Is that what you want? "

"Is that so wrong? "

"Then this may interest you." Lance handed an official-looking document to Ethan.

"This is my financial statement, Ethan. Please note the monetary value of my property holdings in England, all of which I've put up for sale."

Ethan scanned the page with disbelieving eyes, then his eyebrows lifted in surprise. "I never would have guessed. I thought you were poor. But actors don't make this kind of money! Where did you get it? "

"An inheritance. Now, does this change your mind? "

"Not really."

Ethan flung his newspaper to the floor, then he raised himself angrily from his chair and pushed Lance with his fist.

"I don't like you, Maycroft! I never did! "

Lance remained calm. "I don't care if you like me or not." Lance took a deep breath. "Well now, Ethan, where does that leave us? Apparently my financial status doesn't impress you, so let me appeal to your logic. Do you really love your sister or are you concerned with your own financial interests? You could be rich if you chose the right husband for her. Admit it, Ethan. Her happiness means nothing to you."

My brother muttered under his breath. "Bastard!"

"You and I have only one thing in common, Ethan. We both love Elizabeth, so let the wedding proceed without any further trouble, and please understand this. By marrying me, your sister is not abandoning you. That's the one thing you fear most, isn't it?" Ethan's mouth turned grim, tightening into a thin line as he ignored Lance and stared at me with icy eyes.

"Do you want to marry this man, Elizabeth? "

"Yes, I do." My voice was a whisper.

"Then marry him! I won't stop you! But don't come crawling to me when he throws you away!"

With those words, Ethan stalked out of the room, leaving his tension hanging in the air like an evil black cloud.

When we heard Ethan's bedroom door slam shut, Lance took me into his arms. His voice broke as he whispered, "I'm afraid Ethan might do something terrible if you stay here tonight. *Please stay with my sister. You'll be safe with her.*"

"Don't worry, Lance. I'll be fine. I'll keep my bedroom door locked all night, and by tomorrow morning, Ethan will have calmed down." I reached up and held his face in my small hands. He kissed me passionately, then he pushed himself away. "I'd better go now. Lock your door. I'll let myself out."

I could hear the frustration in his voice as he whispered through my locked door, "Until tomorrow, Elizabeth . . ."

Then *tomorrow* became *today.* My wedding day. The sweetest wedding gifts of all had come from my new husband, an exquisite white wedding gown of lavish Victorian lace, a bridal headdress with a long veil, and white silk shoes adorned with little pearls. As I dressed for the happiest moment in my life, I lifted my gown high over my head and let it slide over my nearly-naked body. My skin trembled under its silky touch and the reflection I saw in my bedroom mirror pleased me.

Like an illusion in lavish white Victorian lace, the gown's bodice was tight across my breasts and curved around my waist and over my hips, molding me into a living sculpture. And when I left my bedroom, I didn't go into the parlor, because I knew I'd find Ethan there, sulking and brooding. Instead, I wandered into my studio. And there in the hushed stillness, I danced to a silent song in my heart, my bridal gown billowing out as I whirled around and around.

The Guardian Of Dreams exists here.

Just then, I saw the horse-drawn carriage stopping outside. I waved to the coachman and ran to the parlor to get Ethan. The parlor door squeaked slightly as I opened it, but he was so absorbed in his own thoughts he hadn't heard it.

He was dressed in his best suit, but his hair was tousled and he hadn't shaved.

His eyes looked out of the window, but clearly, they saw nothing. His brow was more deeply furrowed than usual and the corners of his mouth had taken a downward turn. His depression filled the air with a heavy gloom. I took a deep breath and my wedding gown rustled slightly as I entered the room. Ethan turned quickly at the sudden sound.

His smile was quick. "Elizabeth! I've never seen you look so beautiful!" He moved toward me, then quickly put his hands on my shoulders. His eyes betrayed him.

"Elizabeth, don't marry him! I need you more than he does!" His grip tightened.

"Please don't do this, Ethan."

"Then I won't be at your wedding!"

He angrily picked up his suitcase by the door, then he paused in the open doorway, speaking in his usual sarcastic tone. "Don't worry, I'll keep my promise to stay with friends for three weeks. I certainly don't want to hear Maycroft's grunts and groans when you're in bed together!"

He slammed the door behind him, rattling all the pictures on the walls. But I couldn't worry about Ethan's anger . . .

I had a wedding to go to. *Mine.*

Minutes later, I was walking down the long church aisle toward my new husband, and soon, we were side by side, our hands touching in a secret pledge as we exchanged our vows.

We never took our eyes from each other as we repeated our promise. As Lance slipped the sparkling wedding band on my finger, his touch was like a lightning-shock, full of fire and intense love. But when the pastor said "until death do you part," a chill shot through me like a mile-long shaft of ice.

There was no logical reason for the terror I felt, but it disappeared without a trace when I heard, "I now pronounce you husband and wife." Then the pastor whispered to Lance with a fatherly smile.

"You may kiss your bride, young man."

Lance raised my bridal veil.

He took me into his arms, secretly melting me with his touch as my trembling lips met his in a discreet public kiss.

Through Lance's tuxedo jacket, I could feel his heart pounding, matching my own heart, beat for beat. Alone in our private world of two, our wedding kiss seemed endless until the pastor tapped Lance on the shoulder.

"That's lovely, dear boy, but your friends are waiting for you." We smiled at the pastor, then merged into the crowd of friends and wedding guests.

As we left for the reception, the pastor called out, "Bless you, my children. A long life and happiness to you both!" And later, the pastor repeated those words at the wedding reception.

Lance had hired the ballroom at the finest hotel in New York and all of our friends celebrated our marriage in the midst of fragrant summer flowers and candlelit elegance. Everyone was there . . . Lance's sister Anne, all the actors and actresses from his theatrical troupe, and my ballet patrons, generous people who had given us lavish wedding gifts.

In a special Shakespearean tribute, my new husband raised his glass of champagne in a wedding toast.

"To my bride's beauty and virgin innocence. She is a poet's dream." As we sipped the sparkling golden liquid, Lance watched me with half-closed eyes over the top of his champagne glass, sending silent promises of passion to come.

And so, surrounded by all the people who were so dear to us, the next few hours passed quickly — hours filled with laughter, merriment and dancing.

It was perfect.

Lance and I danced a Viennese waltz around the entire ballroom to the accompaniment of the fine orchestra Lance had hired for the occasion. As we whirled past the entrance, I saw Ethan coming through the huge oak doors.

Lance stepped in front of me.

"Stay behind me, Elizabeth." Then he stood his ground firmly as Ethan steadily moved toward us. Without warning, my brother gripped Lance's hand in a gentleman's handshake and spoke low.

"You win, Maycroft. Just be sure you take good care of my sister." *It sounded more like a warning.* Then Ethan kissed me on the cheek, whispering so low that only I could hear him.

"I was wrong, dear Elizabeth." He put his arms around me. "Sometimes, I think I love you too much."

His body trembled against mine and his tears wet my cheek. *I never saw Ethan cry before today.*

Then he turned away and left.

Lance held me as I wept, too. But soon, in a hidden corner of the ballroom, Lance whispered, "It's time to go." His breath on my face was warm and sweet.

Like a divine fire touching my cheek . . .

Moments later, we hurried to our waiting carriage with its coachman and two fine white horses.

Their silvery manes swayed in the wind as we sped away into the night to be together.

For the first time.

Chapter 4:

NIGHT OF NEW PASSIONS

Our wedding night — my initiation into a secret world so long denied to me — was only minutes away. Tonight, our passions would be set free and I would finally be *his*.

As the horse-drawn carriage carried us home swiftly, Lance whispered to me of all the intimate pleasures he would show me this night. Throughout our engagement, our subdued passions have been an explosion waiting to happen, making our physical desires difficult to control, but we did, and that's what made this night so special.

The horses stopped at the coachman's command.

We were home.

We exchanged knowing glances as the coachman helped Lance gather my gown's long train so that it wouldn't touch the sidewalk. Then my husband swept me up into his arms and carried me across the dimly-lit threshold, pressing his mouth against mine in a kiss that promised much more. And when he left to pay the carriage driver, I wandered into our bedroom.

Dozens of candles awaited their flames and the aroma of fresh flowers became the perfume of stars. Fluffy pillows rose high on our wedding-bed of softest eider-down while new bed-linens wafted the fresh scent of early-morning sunshine.

My small hand trembled as I lit the candles and my heart was beating so fast I thought I'd die as I moved quickly to close the new curtains. Then I looked around the room.

It was the most romantic of settings.

When Lance walked through the doorway, I saw all of his powerful passions shining from his eyes, passions that would find their relief this night, this long-awaited night. In the glow of candlelight, his gaze adored me, worshipped me, *excited me* as he took my face in his hands and kissed my cheeks, my closed eyes and my lips. His voice was deep with urgency and his gaze was so intense that it seemed to penetrate me with its familiar longing.

"Tonight, Elizabeth, I will love you as no man has ever loved a woman before."

Then he held me without speaking. We were beyond words. My virgin body was not afraid of him, nor of this first time, not afraid of his man's touch . . .

Secret places in me came alive and eagerly responded to him as he parted my lips and explored my mouth in an exotic new way. How my body ached for him . . . he had lit a fire in me and made it blaze with his strong male hands moving over my clothed body, as if memorizing my curves.

Then suddenly, he swept me up into his arms as if I were weightless and carried me to our wedding bed. My eyelashes trembled against his cheek and my feminine curves molded to the hypnotic contours of his body.

His breath warmed my cheek and I gave myself freely to his passionate kisses and the forbidden intimacy of his secret touch. He wrapped me in his aura of invisible warmth and I trusted him completely.

As he gently laid me down on our wedding bed, he covered my soft mouth with the moist warmth of his kisses. Endless and deep, they quickly stirred my passion to new heights. Every inch of my flesh was on fire as his breath grew hot and deep and vibrated within me.

My new husband undressed me slowly, worshipfully, until I was totally naked before him. His eyes shone with approval as they raked over my entire body, from my firm breasts and the valley between, to my small waist curving into my hips, over veiled and secret places to my long legs and slender ankles. Unashamed, I watched as he undressed himself and moved into our bed, close to me.

His life's breath warmed me and inflamed me, and I could see the rising warmth of his manly body.

I felt his hot skin touching mine.

And with his hands, long-fingered and strong, he took my small hands and guided them to himself, inviting me to explore the newness and the wonder of him.

My breath quickened with the discovery.

Firm beneath my hesitant fingertips, his muscles tensed even further under my whisper-light touch and he reacted to my caress with a long audible moan.

In the candlelight's glow, I gazed at Lance's form with the awe and adoration of a woman who had never seen a virile naked man before. His body was firm, slim and manly, and to me, he resembled a god of ancient myths.

His physique was that of a marble Greek statue, perfectly proportioned and artistically powerful. I was mesmerized as I watched his potent body respond to his mind's commands.

And while I had been admiring his maleness, he had been studying me with half-closed eyes, from my long wavy hair to my delicate feet and all the intimate inches in between.

Then I surrendered completely to his mastery.

His virile touch was magic, as powerful as a summer storm, but his searching mouth was erotic as he explored my warmed flesh, searing a sensuous pathway down my throat and shoulders to all the secret places beyond. His fiery mouth covered me with forbidden kisses, moist and enticing, leading me down the pathway to ecstasy. Soon my whole body was aflame and I was pleading for more.

His most intimate kiss was volcanic. Secluded regions of my virgin body came alive with dazzling new sensations as his mouth explored me in forbidden ways. Mysterious passions flared through me and my honey flowed like liquid fire as his passionate mouth caressed my hot flesh, but he restrained himself until he knew the time was right.

He asked me, in a whisper, if I was ready.

I whispered, "*Yes, oh yes . . .*"

I gasped as he lowered his body into mine. He moaned as I welcomed him eagerly into my flesh, and tears trickled down my cheeks as my virgin blood flowed. I was no longer a virgin.

He laid still until my pain passed, then he began to move inside of me, gentle at first. As my honey flowed freely from me, his probing thrusts intensified until he was driving deeper and deeper into me, his gasping breath blowing hot across my face each time he thrust himself into me, delighting in the passions he had aroused in my virginal body. Deeper and deeper he went, faster and faster, harder and harder.

He whispered to me of his love, of even more secrets he would reveal to me, more forbidden lusts we would share.

My cries of ecstasy echoed on the perfumed air.

Finally, our bodies thrashed together as our imprisoned passions demanded their climax and he pressed his mouth against mine at the summit of my sensual awakening.

A billion stars exploded inside of me, coursing through us where we were joined together. My flesh *there* throbbed and pulsated as great waves of passion consumed me.

I screamed out his name as if he were a god.

With a great moan, his own passion claimed its reward and he erupted like a volcano inside of me, merging with me in the intensity of our passion. His rhythmic pulsations sent more throbbing waves through me, *again,* and I moaned wildly as new lightning burned through us with scorching-hot embers.

The skies part. The core of the earth melts.

Love flowed between us like warmed honey and softly-spoken words of love penetrated the air around us, just as he had penetrated me, body and soul.

I have never felt more alive.

Afterward, I saw adoration in his gaze, and as he rested, I watched his masculine chest rise and fall with each new breath while he regained his strength for the hours to come. We looked into each other's eyes, *and he knew.* My flesh was on fire again, eager for the probing lust of his potent flesh and the touch of his magical hands. Soon, his mouth was on me again with a fierce hunger that matched my own.

In only a few short hours, Lance has transformed me from a shy virgin into a seductive temptress.

I savor the change he has made in me.

In the weeks and months that followed, we burned with a sexual hunger that only the other could satisfy. I was more like Lance's mistress than his wife and he was my lover.

And each night, new pleasures awaited us.

At the summit of our passion, he would have to press his mouth hard against mine so Ethan wouldn't hear us, then we'd muffle each other's moans, riding the waves of passion until we were breathless and exhausted.

I drank him in like fine wine and begged for more.

Chapter 5:

THE LURE OF DISTANT HORIZONS

December entered our lives with a blustery storm.

During the four months since my marriage, a tentative peace has been established with my brother. A fragile peace.

But happily, Christmas is coming, and while I decorated the house in a holiday mood, I was hiding a wonderful secret, one I couldn't reveal until I was sure.

But now, something else was giving me hope ... for many months, we've been hearing about California, Oregon and other western territories. Adventurers, fur trappers and old mountain men brought back glorious tales of wondrous places, rich land with trees so tall they grew right through the clouds. Pioneers by the hundreds were joining the westward emigration, urged by our government's promise of free land and new lives. Skies as blue as the finest sapphires are said to exist there ... plush green velvet landscapes glowing with wildflowers, a farmer's paradise with soil so rich it blackened everything it touched, blessed by a bountiful sun and reliable rainfall.

A paradise on earth, they said, and I pictured our new home on America's frontier, trellised with roses and clustered with emerald ivy climbing up to the roof. Surely our dreams could come true in such an extraordinary place, along with a new future filled with adventure and vision.

We weren't the only ones driven by the hunger for a new life in the western territories. All people with unfulfilled dreams were joining the wagon trains. Farmers journeyed from many nations to join the long pioneer caravans — dairy farmers from the Scandinavian countries, potato farmers from Ireland and others from faraway lands, including Germany and Lance's England. Courageous caravans carved a visible trail toward sundown, pointing the way west and taming raw land as they traveled. We've heard terrible stories of the dangers they've encountered and we knew that death waited for many of us who dared to attempt the journey, but tales of successful journeys were the only ones that held our attention, especially with our new financial difficulties. Lance was not as famous in America as he had been in Europe, but he put his impressive talent to work by teaching evening drama classes and he also worked long days at Ethan's place of employment.

Ethan was enjoying his role as Lance's boss, but although Lance never complained to me, I could see the strain showing on his face. Every day in our little home, annoyance floated in the air like a black cloud. The closeness in which we had to live was too crowded and confining for three people who didn't get along. Each dawn brought new arguments and hostilities.

One night before going to sleep, I pleaded with my husband, "We need a new life, Lance. Pastor Wesley is joining one of the wagon trains leaving in the Spring. Couldn't we go, too?" He held me, but I'd already seen *no* written on his face.

"Elizabeth, you know I want to, but until we get the money from the sale of my home in England, we can't afford it. And if we try and fail, our situation will be far worse than it already is." He pulled me closer to him and whispered, "We have to consider the dangers. Make no mistake about it, my love. There's death out there." His terrifying words had silenced me for the moment, yet, with each passing day, we continued to hear the most amazing tales and exciting stories, tempting us, seducing us with their invisible promises. Lance and I glanced at each other, but did not speak.

Who would suggest it first, I wondered . . .

But loving my new husband took away the uncertainty of daily life. Many evenings, though, we needed the rooms to ourselves so that we could express our passion without fear of being overheard. At those tense times, I would respectfully ask Ethan if he was planning to go out to see friends, perhaps?

Ethan always saw through my little charade, but he would grudgingly leave for an hour or two. It made him very angry to hear my new husband and I making love on the other side of his bedroom wall. But in the heat of passion, I couldn't keep silent. My sighs of pleasure soon turned to joyful moans, and in my final ecstasy, I would scream Lance's name.

But we didn't know that Ethan sometimes returned early. When morning came, Ethan's annoyance always told us that he had been in the house last night, listening, perhaps watching.

Ethan was so quiet, he seemed to walk on cat's feet.

Ethan's resentment toward Lance had not disappeared, as we hoped it would, and our relationship with him was at the breaking point. Late one night, minutes after Lance and I had made love and were drifting off to sleep, I heard a thumping noise coming from just outside our bedroom door. *Probably a shutter blowing in the wind*, I thought. I arose from bed and walked to the door, but when I opened it, I saw Ethan standing there, hunched over. I gasped at what he was doing.

Lance bolted out of bed, naked and furious. He brushed past me and grabbed Ethan, then he pushed Ethan hard against the wall and smashed him in the mouth with his closed fist. Ethan crumpled to the floor, holding his jaw and staring at me as I cried. Ethan had never seen me naked before.

The look in my brother's eyes made me feel ashamed, and I tried unsuccessfully to cover myself with my hands. Then Lance hurried me back into our room, slammed the door shut and locked it. The following day, nerves were strained and tempers flared. The incident had only made things worse.

But as we three tried to mend our hurt feelings, the outside world intruded with frightening headlines. Widespread epidemics of cholera and scarlet fever were sweeping the land and we lived in constant fear as the infectious diseases raged through the world's cities and countrysides, leaving thousands dead in their path. My students have dwindled in number, along with our income.

Weeks passed slowly. Newspaper headlines grew larger.

One morning at breakfast, I had to say what we were all thinking. "Why don't we go west," I said in a half-whisper, then I sipped my tea and watched the two men's faces over the rim of my teacup. My brother looked at me as if I'd lost my mind, but a consenting smile was spreading across my husband's face. His hand eagerly reached for mine under the lace tablecloth and as his grasp tightened lovingly, I could see the hunger for a fresh start in his eyes. "Yes, my love! That's where our answer lies!" Lance paused, then turned to Ethan. "Will you be joining us? "

Ethan ignored him and slammed his fist on the table, then he stared hard at me. The veins on his temples bulged out and throbbed with each word he spoke. "Do you know what you're saying? I'd have to give up a good position!" He shook his head." And I'm certainly not willing to throw away my savings on some foolish journey to the middle of nowhere!"

I ignored his sarcastic tone. "But Ethan, just imagine the perfect life that waits for us there. Lance's property will be sold soon, I can sell Mother's jewelry, and you can sell your . . ." Ethan's angry eyes warned me to stop, but I added a few more temptations. "You can start your own business. *That's something you've always wanted.* You may even find a fine wife who'll make you happy, and we'll have more space to live in. Oh, Ethan, wouldn't it be wonderful!" But Ethan ignored us, pretending to read his newspaper. Then Lance's grip tightened on my hand and he nodded toward Ethan. I followed his gaze.

I had to smile. Ethan's newspaper was upside-down.

Lance continued to hold my hand under the table as we watched Ethan finish his breakfast. Still, he said nothing to us and angrily pushed his chair away from the table. As he stood, Ethan's eyes met mine, and for an instant, I saw the flicker of consent there. But so was the anger, and he left the house quickly, mumbling something about being late for work.

Actually, he was early.

But even though our relationship with my brother was not a happy one, Ethan was our solid rock, the one person in the world who could keep our feet on the ground. Lance and I were often in a romantic world of our own and we didn't think sensibly most of the time.

Ethan was our voice of reason.

Lance finished his breakfast, then glanced at my pale skin with great concern, touching my forehead and both of my cheeks. "You don't feel feverish, Elizabeth, but you seem ill. Something is wrong. I'll get the doctor!" He started to rise, but I put my hand on his and smiled with a secret smile, then I confessed. "I'll give you your special Christmas present now. I've had the morning sickness for a while now, but I won't be sure until I see the doctor on the day before Christmas." *He grinned. He already knew what I was going to say.* "Merry Christmas, Lance. Your first prince or princess is on the way."

"Elizabeth, this is the most wonderful Christmas present you could have given me! But don't tell Ethan yet. He may not take the news well and I want to be there when he finds out."

And so, we decided not to tell Ethan our secret yet.

Days later, Lance and I decided to sell the rest of our valuable possessions to finance the westward journey, but Lance's sacrifice would be the greatest. He would part with his rapier, the short-bladed 18th century sword which had been in his family for well over 100 years. It was an extremely valuable antique, the only family heirloom that Lance kept with him wherever he traveled. It was also the most exquisite thing I'd ever seen. I knew the inner impact of Lance's sacrifice, but he knew that the sword would command a high price, particularly since it was sheathed in a solid gold scabbard studded with diamonds, emeralds, rubies and many other gems.

Before we were married, Lance wanted to pry the largest diamonds from the golden scabbard just to have a lovely diamond necklace made for me, but I wouldn't let him. I loved him enough to keep his treasure intact.

I didn't need expensive jewelry. I had Lance.

But even with the jeweler's high appraisal and a firm offer to buy the antique sword at a very generous price, we still didn't have enough money to pay for our westward journey.

Now it was my turn to sacrifice. I would have to sell the jewelry I inherited from my mother after her death. As I gently touched each one, I was sad to realize that I wouldn't be able to pass them on to the daughters that Lance and I might have in the future. He watched me silently as I held each one up to the light. "Keep your favorites, Elizabeth, for your little girls."

And so, I kept the most beautiful jewels and parted with the rest, but we were still short of the money we needed. We approached my brother again, but still, Ethan would not agree.

At that moment, my husband and I made a decision. If Ethan would not come with us, we'd embark on our dangerous journey without him. We would leave, just the two of us, with only our love to keep us alive.

Somehow, we'd learn to survive in the wilderness.

We'd build our paradise out of dust, if we had to.

But on a snowy Christmas Eve, two landmark events took place. The doctor confirmed that our first baby will be born in the spring. And Ethan said *yes*.

Tonight, Lance, Ethan and I will celebrate Christmas Eve with a candlelit dinner at New York's finest restaurant.

I plan to tell my brother about the baby tonight.

Dinner was perfection, and during dessert, I cautiously whispered, "I'm going to have a baby in the springtime. Please don't be angry, Ethan." I leaned back in my chair and waited.

He grew deathly quiet, then he showed us a broad smile.

"I'm not a monster, Elizabeth. And I may not be a father, but it looks like I *am* going to be an uncle, *a proud one.*"

He congratulated Lance with a cool handshake, then he leaned close to me and held my face in his brotherly hands as his voice grew softer. "You're going to be a wonderful mother, my dear, dear Elizabeth." Then he kissed me gently.

For the first time in our lives.

January's storms were blown away by February winds, whipping across the city in stormy gusts. As the baby grew within me, I became easily chilled and I would shiver from the cold. Ethan would always bolt out of his chair, put more logs on the fire, then he'd wrap me up in blankets and warm my hands with his own breath. *The baby has completely changed Ethan. He's very loving now and very attentive to my needs.*

The two men in my life made sure that I ate only the most wholesome foods, and their sweet concern for my health kept me warm through winter's bitter cold. Whenever I was alone, I'd daydream, visualizing our peaceful frontier home, a place where dreams are born and fulfilled, a place that will sing with the laughter of children. Just then, I felt my baby kick.

My curvaceous body became much more womanly as the unborn baby grew within me. Nature's milk filled my proud breasts, making them more voluptuous than ever before.

Lance tells me I have a constant glow, and he loves to gaze at my nakedness. Sometimes before the loving, sometimes after the loving, we'd lay on our bed and Lance would rest his head on my breasts while his gentle hands wandered over my naked flesh, feeling his unborn baby move under his touch.

But one night, when we were alone in the parlor, Lance's voice filled with excitement. "We must choose a name for the child, Elizabeth. Your time is growing near." It was then I learned Lance's lifelong wish and delicious secret.

"I've always wanted to name my sons after kings."

He smiled broadly, but it was more of a grin and I smiled warmly at the gleam I saw in his eyes. "That's a fine idea, my love." I touched his hand with mine, and suddenly, he stood tall and erect, with a courtly bow. "Your own name is that of a queen. Elizabeth, the only child born to King Henry the Eighth and the tragic young Anne Boleyn." When I protested, he quieted me with a kiss. "But you are *my* Elizabeth. You will always be *my* queen." His kiss led to more passionate touching.

Hours later, we resumed our quest and entered into an amazingly simple agreement. I will name our daughters. He will name our sons. Lance was anxious to hear my choices, and he was pleased with my first choice. Purity, a popular name of our times . . . she'd be a sweet child, a gentle little lady hostessing tea parties for all her little dolls. The next girl's name pleased him greatly and his smile softened into a kiss, just for me. Our second daughter will be named Anne, for Lance's sweet sister. As for Lance's choices, they were regal. "Richard, for Richard the Lion-Hearted." His moist eyes were appealing as he spoke. "I shall call him 'Lion-Heart' for his inborn courage." Then he continued his list of very carefully chosen king's names. "Charles, James, Edward . . ."

We agreed on all names except that of Henry. The name sent an icy chill through me. The reason would not be known to me for many, many years, but I would eventually learn why the name of Henry the Eighth, the beheader of unwanted wives, had frightened me so.

I pleaded without explaining.

"Please, any name except Henry."

He quickly omitted the name from his list with the cooperative flick of his pen and the words, "So it is done, my lady." Then he smiled and leaned close, kissing me in his own special way. Lance could make even the simplest moments of our lives dramatic and full of excitement.

The clock chimed.

We looked sorrowfully at each other, sharing the sad disappointment of having to part on this happiest of days, but our conversation drew to a hurried close as he prepared to leave for his performance at the theater a few streets away from here.

How I loved to look at him . . . he was perfection itself.

Grasping his cape, he lifted it high above his head and whirled it onto his wide shoulders. Then he wrapped it around both of us and pressed me close to him, kissing me deeply with his probing mouth. And with a smile, he was gone. My heart always went out the door with him, returning only when he came home to me.

Lance's presence in New York had inspired a renewed interest in Shakespearean plays, with Lance portraying the lead role in *HAMLET*. He hired the best actors he could find for all the other parts, and at the end of each performance, the theater owner paid Lance a percentage of the profits. It helped us to buy what we needed for our hazardous journey westward.

We tried to time everything very carefully so that we'd reach Independence, Missouri, by our wagon train's departure date. But we also worried about our baby's birth.

Our first baby will enter this world surrounded by a barren wilderness, somewhere along the pioneer trail. I've had no assurance that a medical doctor will be traveling with our wagon train, but I hope I'll be fortunate and find someone who will attend me when my time comes.

But in this moment, alone and lonely, my thoughts returned to Lance.

The source of my strength, the purpose of my life . . .

Shadows lengthened and darkened the cobblestoned view outside our frosty windows as I watched and waited for my husband's return.

Suddenly, a figure appeared in the distance holding a bright light. It was Noel, the new lamplighter.

"A pleasant chap," Lance had called the man who came each evening at dusk to light the street lamps and push away the darkness.

At the instant Noel touched his golden flame to the lamp, it transformed our little corner of the world *as if by magic* into a fairytale scene from a child's storybook — colorful, warm and innocent. The gas-lamp flickered and danced inside of its delicate glass enclosure as a March snowfall swept over New York, buffeted by the unforgiving wind.

In the quiet hush of my loneliness, my body throbbed and ached for my husband's eager touch. Then the familiar rush of desire swept through my fertile body as I remembered Lance's skill and our never-ending passions.

I needed him.

I needed him *now* . . . my body craved him and my mouth hungered for the taste of him.

Quickly, I opened my notebook, the hiding-place of my secret and forbidden thoughts, hidden from all eyes except *his*. My hand trembled as I wrote with the pretty plumed pen Lance bought for me, just yesterday.

Ice-blue sequined snow glistens beneath the night sky as I wait for you, my only love. Cathedrals and crystal palaces surround me and an audible silence echoes in the mirrors of my mind. Fragile snowflakes float through the small window-panes. They kiss my face, my cheeks, my closed eyes, my lips, the way you always do. Where are you now? Nearby, yes, I know. Yet you are so very far from my reach.

I glance at the time. The wedding-gift clock is my enemy until the sweet hour of your return. My misty eyes search through the swirling veil of snowflakes and I wait — and wait. Finally, I see you through the snowfall, hurrying back to me with your long, quick stride — your cape blowing in the March wind. Suddenly you're here, my love, and the sunny warmth of summer comes home with you.

My book fell to the carpet as I heard Lance's key turn in the lock. I ran to him and rushed into his open arms.

I barely felt the chill from his snow-covered cape.

He dropped the wet cape from his shoulders.

As it fell to the floor, he swept me up into his arms, whirling me around and around in a joyous dance, sweetening the air around us with laughter and honeyed sounds.

Suddenly, the dance stopped.

Our bodies had warmed quickly in response to our rising passions and he took my mouth in a wild, untamed kiss.

No one would guess that this refined gentleman, a most singular man who possessed a king's courtly manners, was such a passionate lover, so eager to please.

And in pleasing me, he pleased himself.

I rested my head on his shoulder.

He carried me into our bedroom and laid me down gently, as if I were a breakable doll made of fine china. Then he closed the door and snapped the new lock shut, quickly undressing himself as he returned to me.

His loving mouth covered me with moist kisses as he stripped me under the blankets until we were both naked.

Within moments, our trembling bodies were intertwined, locked together in passion's fire.

Chapter 6:

TOWARD SUNDOWN

Springtime came with a whisper and we were finally at the starting point of our journey, Independence, Missouri. We arrived only a few days before embarking on our journey. Lance's sister has chosen to stay in New York to pursue a career on the stage, so we are three in number — Lance, Ethan and I.

2,000 miles of raw land stretched out before us like a giant's beckoning hand, tempting us and seducing us with its promise and its unlimited dreams. We knew that death awaited some of us in that frontier Eden, but we had the courage to follow our wildest dreams and most fanciful imaginings. The possibility that our daydreams could turn into a nightmare was never discussed. *The journey* was the most important reality.

The journey. What wondrous words!

An intense thrill sparkled in the air as hundreds of pioneers prepared for the journey. We treasured every hour, guarding each minute and using it well. But it seemed that time raced too quickly for all that had to be done, and leisurely conversations were a luxury none of us could afford to indulge in. The Captain visited each wagon, assigned a specific place in the long wagon-line, and paused for a friendly talk with each of us, confirming destinations and ending with a firm request that we'd maintain our position in the long line until we reach journey's end. Captain Taylor's easy smile and relaxed manner made us feel welcome. But now, he's staring at my stomach.

"Well, little lady, it looks like you'll be needing a midwife soon." He saw my disappointment with the word *midwife*.

"I'm sorry, ma'am. There's no doctor on this wagon train, but we do have an expert midwife two wagons ahead of yours. And you'll be glad to hear that she's traveling with some young midwives-in-training. I'll arrange for you to meet Mrs. Holm before we head out." Then his voice grew gentle. "Don't worry, little lady. Kirsten Holm is rumored to have healing hands."

The following day, I rested on my bed, patiently waiting for Mrs. Holm. *Fear filled me . . . my timing couldn't have been worse.* At that moment, I heard Lance and Ethan greeting the midwife and assisting her as she climbed the steps, then they waited outside.

Silhouetted against the deep-blue afternoon sky, I saw my visitor, a lovely old silver-haired woman. Compassion shone through each fold and furrow of her aged face, but when she smiled, the years dropped away and she was as young as a girl.

"I'm here to answer your questions and ease your fears, Elizabeth. But right now, let me examine you and check on your baby's well-being." Her touch was gentle and there was no pain. When she finished, her voice was a whisper.

"Elizabeth dear, your baby seems fully developed and active, so if it's born early, it *will* survive. My only concern is for you. You're remarkably small, down there. You'll suffer more than other women, but I'll do everything in my power to ease your pain and make your first birthing easier. There are ways, not very pleasant, but there are ways to ease the baby's path to the outside world. My assistants and I are always near, just two wagons forward, and we'll attend you when your time comes. If you feel any sudden pain, have your husband or brother run and get me right away! If it's nighttime, tell them to wake me!" Then she patiently answered my questions. Since the wagon train could not come to a halt for birth, our hope is that the baby will come during one of our overnight stops. If it happens over the jolting wagon-wheels, the wagon will roll and pitch, tossing us like rag dolls. The baby and I would die.

She smiled as she prepared to leave.

"I know that the start of our journey is going to be an exciting time for you, but please try to stay calm. Whenever the wagon is rolling, lie in bed on your side." But one look at my face revealed my desire to sit on the wooden seat up front so I could see everything. Then she laughed in a good-natured way and warned me as she left. "Then sit on pillows!"

I knew I was in good hands . . . *healing hands*.

"Wake up, Elizabeth. Today is the day!" Lance's waking kiss warmed me and I stretched like a pampered Persian kitten.

We've waited so very long for this day — the start of our pioneer journey. Under a clear sky and bright sunshine, a trail scout on horseback galloped along the expanse of haphazardly-placed wagons, making sure we were all awake. His shouts couldn't fail to awaken us.

"After your morning meal we'll get your wagons in line, then we'll start to roll!" were shouted to each pioneer family.

But putting the wagons in the properly numbered order proved to be nearly impossible. Oxen's harnesses tangled and as the reins slipped out of drivers' hands, the oxen went in the wrong direction. *It was chaos.*

Covered wagons bumped into each other as hundreds of pioneers tried to maneuver their wagons into the long line. Damaged wagons had to be quickly repaired or risk being left behind, along with their owners. Fights broke out along the long line of wagons, and Captain Taylor's voice could be heard shouting orders to his men. They confirmed his orders, then shot their rifles into the air. The fighting stopped.

Several horses broke loose from the rear.

Wild, strong and free, how magnificent they were! I was thrilled as I watched the defiant horses try to evade capture. Their tails thrashed as they reared up, pawing the air, their nostrils flaring with the sweet scent of freedom. But one by one, they were finally herded back by the trail-scouts. I saw the horses' eyes as they passed by our wagon. The glimmer of freedom was still there!

Following obediently at the end of the wagon train were large herds of livestock — cattle mostly, and yoked teams of brawny oxen. There were mules and horses, too, with hired hands to keep the animals from straying.

Pastor Wesley's wagon pulled ahead and his family waved cheerfully as he tried to maneuver his wagon past ours, but his wagon wheel grazed ours and nearly tipped our wagon over. I started to fall and grabbed onto one of the hickory bows, but my fingers slipped off. Luckily, Lance caught me in time and he held me as the pastor called out an embarrassed apology. Hours later, all our wagons were in line.

The line that would reach clear across America.

Morning slowly turned into afternoon, then twilight came fast, and while we waited, Lance, Ethan and I talked about the months of feverish preparations and all the fascinating things we've acquired. The covered wagon and yoked oxen had been our biggest expenses. We've also bought two horses and a little goat named Bluebell, named for the little bell around her neck.

Our wagon was picturesque and cozy, a combination parlor, bedroom and kitchen. Its huge canvas cover was tightly stretched over enormous rounded hickory bows, with pucker ropes at both ends to provide protection against sudden storms and prying eyes. The wagon's cover was cleverly designed so that we could roll it back for cooler air when we travel through the prairie's scorching heat. And with heavy cords, Lance and Ethan had secured the two treasures I cannot leave behind.

The first was as necessary to me as food, my little piano, where I find nourishment of a different kind. The other, a large mirror from my ballet studio. It's not vanity which made me want to take the mirror. Mirrors were nearly impossible to find on the frontier and the mirror served a practical purpose. Inside the crowded wagon, the mirror visually doubled our space, making it *seem* more spacious than it really was.

Every moment was precious. If all goes well, we'll spend several months in the crossing of this land. If all does not go well, or if we're seriously delayed by harsh weather or other disasters, the trip will take much longer and could mean death for many of us. We'd all been instructed to take only the barest essentials . . . an ample supply of food, water casks, medicines, cookware and other necessities such as bedding, pillows and quilts. We've also brought clothes for the new baby, some of Ethan's scholarly books, my ballet costumes, a few books of poetry (including *The Raven* by Edgar Allan Poe,) *Wuthering Heights* and new sunbonnets to protect my fragile skin from the bright prairie sunshine. With farming tools strapped to the wagon's exterior, we were prepared for almost anything. We've also brought sturdy leather clothing for Lance and Ethan. How handsome they'll look in their new fringed buckskin shirts and trousers just like the trail scouts and mountain men wear. And hanging from small hooks is a tiny cradle, waiting for the new baby . . . handmade by Lance and Ethan, two men who had never built anything with their hands before.

We've brought our dreams, too. *They take no space at all.*
We're already one day behind schedule.

Nightfall is coming fast. It has taken the entire morning and afternoon to form the single line of wagons. We'll have to wait until tomorrow's sunrise to begin our journey.

In my excitement, I couldn't sleep that night, but I was content to rest in the protection of Lance's arms and think about tomorrow. Despite the difficulties we faced, this would be an adventure we'd never forget.

Soon it was morning and the weather was perfection. Sunlight shone brightly in a cloudless sky. After finishing breakfast, we readied ourselves for the journey.

Oxen snorted and pawed the ground while burnished horses shook their manes in the pale morning light. We waited for our signal, then we heard a rifle-shot somewhere in the front of the line and the team-master's whip snapping hard.

Captain Taylor shouted out, "WAGONS HO," then his wagon moved out, followed by the rest of us. Our happy shouts rang from one end of the line to the other. Rising excitement raced through the caravan and we all cheered as we wheeled toward sundown. Happy shouts of all the young men on horseback, galloping way out in front, merged with the sound of turning wagon-wheels. I was so happy.

My heart was like a runaway horse, fast and free. From my well-cushioned perch on the pillows, I watched as Lance led the oxen by the leather strap he'd connected to their yoke.

Ethan walked side-by-side with Lance and I was warmed by the friendship that was finally growing between them. Lance smiled and called out to me. "Happy, Elizabeth?" I smiled and nodded an emotional *YES!* I didn't dare speak. I don't want him to see that I've been biting my lip in pain.

With each turn of the huge iron-strapped wheels, my body was jolted and shaken, despite all of the soft pillows underneath me, and I held tightly onto the wooden plank that served as the wagon's front seat.

Most of the people who rode inside the wagons were expectant mothers, children and those who were ill. Most of the men controlled the oxen from the front seat, rode horses, or, like Lance and Ethan, walked across America.

During the first week, our days fell into a comforting routine. In the beginning, it never varied. Before sunrise, sentinels would fire their rifles into the air to awaken us. Trail scouts would saddle up their horses and gallop out of the circle to check the road ahead, while hired hands headed toward the back of the line. Sleepily, we prepared a quick breakfast and pioneer men yoked their teams of oxen and mules, making sure that the wagons were ready to move out.

A trumpet's blare, somewhere toward the front of the wagon train, announced the start of another day's march. By sundown, we were weary and looked forward to a safe night's rest. We were racing against nature.

I was racing against time.

Whenever Captain Taylor would find a likely location for our overnight stop, he'd halt the wagon train. Then the most experienced men and trail scouts would take over, closing the wagons into an unbroken circle.

Early the following morning, we'd start all over again.

The road we take dared and tempted us with an intriguing arrogance. I dreaded the thousands of rugged miles ahead.

Exact timing could mean the difference between life and a slow death. If we were delayed, we could be closed in by an early winter blizzard, or we could run out of food, as others had done. Clean water may have been polluted by earlier wagon trains and violent weather was a serious possibility. It was a well-known fact that death visited regularly in deepest snowdrifts, while hard-driving rainstorms and slashing sleet had spelled disaster for many who had gone before us.

I dared not think of the dangers from human hands.

We were warned to listen for tribal drums and be ready to pull the wagons into a tight circle at a moment's notice, with or without the help of the trail scouts.

And each day, the Captain would remind us of the deeper significance of our journey. Our courage would be tested, but our strength, and perhaps our valiant deaths, will inspire future generations to conquer their fears and search for their dreams.

They will remember us, he had said. They will remember our sacrifices, our ordeals and our pain.

Springtime had gifted us with lengthening light during this earliest part of our journey. Gentle weather made for joyous times before we're forced to meet the danger that waited for us ... *there ... in the distance, where the land meets the sky.*

It was a difficult journey, and for me, a slow torture. Our wagon jolted and hurtled with punishing momentum as each mile was conquered in search of a dream. Every jarring impact of the wagon's wheels caused me severe pain, and I had to spend most of my days lying on my side in our featherbed to cushion and protect the active child growing within me.

Two weeks into our journey, my labor started.

The sun danced low in the western sky, tinting the clouds with tongues of red fire the night our baby was born. We had left Independence, Missouri, only two weeks ago.

A soft breeze fanned the interior of the wagon as Lance patted my face with a cool cloth and tied my long hair with white satin ribbon from my little sewing box.

As the birth drew near, he held me tight. The sound of his voice comforted me and he was generous with his kisses, until a coiling pain tore my lips from his in a scream. And as the long hours passed, some of the young midwives helped me by propping my upper body on several feather pillows. Although I was reclining, I was almost upright. Mrs. Holm told me that this position would ease the birthing.

"Let Mother Nature do some of the work," she smiled.

Mrs. Holm's skin folded like delicate parchment paper whenever she smiled, but when she looked at Lance now, she wasn't smiling.

Lance's presence was not welcome at this usually-female ritual, and Mrs. Holm tried to send him away.

"This is no place for a man! Go outside!" She made a shoo-ing motion with both hands. "Please, Mr. Maycroft. You shouldn't see your woman like this!"

I tugged on his shirt sleeve.

"Please stay," I whispered. "I'm so frightened."

"I won't leave you, my love. The only place for me is here by your side." Then he fluffed my pillows and ignored the stares of angry midwives.

If the women were worried about my modesty at a time when most married couples made love with their clothes on, they needn't have been concerned. Lance has seen and explored every inch of my flesh and found me a willing subject. He has seen me, and loved me, in the tiniest detail.

He has even looked into my soul.

In the tortured hours that followed, Lance never left my side, but gifted me with his courage and cradled me in his arms during the short time between pains. And all the while, Mrs. Holm massaged my body in downward motions to quicken the birth, while all the young midwives watched and learned from the woman with the healing hands.

He inspired me with his strength and eased my pain with pretty words, soft caresses whispered into my hair, until my final scream, ushered in by another coiling pain that threatened to rip out my insides. At that moment, our first child was born.

A strong, healthy boy, Richard Maycroft cried lustily as he entered this cold world, forced out of his warm, moist domain of several months into an alien environment. "Long live young King Richard," Lance whispered as we studied the innocent pink face of our newborn son. Then he touched my cheek and his love echoed in his words. "And long live the Queen Mother, whom I love with all my heart." He kissed my cheek and caressed my hair as Mrs. Holm reached out for my baby. After cleaning him and wrapping him in blankets, she brought him to me, whispering low of the medical things she must do for me now. *But I knew. I could feel the blood flowing.*

The following week, we heard exciting news.

Logan Halliday,* the legendary explorer and pathfinder, is joining our wagon train soon. He's quite a man, so I've heard, and everyone is anxious to meet him, especially the women.

Some days later, I was taking a short rest in the morning sun while my baby slept and Lance was helping Zeke repair his broken wagon wheel. When I heard women giggling, I knew that Mr. Halliday would be here soon. Suddenly, there he was, walking proudly toward me with Captain Taylor in the lead.

* *Logan Halliday is not his real name.*

Logan Halliday, man of wonders, walked tall, straight and proud, but it was more like a strut, and in his fringed buckskin outfit, he looked every inch like the adventurous man I've heard so much about. Handsome, too, in a rugged sort of way. He moved quickly as they came forward, then the younger man suddenly took the lead away from the much-older Captain, who was trying very hard to keep up with him.

The clean-shaven trail scout stood silently before me.

An easy smile played at the corners of his mouth while flickers of humor leaped from his eyes. Suntanned skin pulled tightly over the ridge of his cheekbones and the lines around his eyes spoke of a lifetime of dangerous adventures.

I sensed a restless power in him.

Masculine wisps of dark chest hair curled through the V of his open shirt, and as he stared at me, we shared a friendly smile. Then his eyes left my face and moved over the rest of me. I quickly put my hands up to my chest, trying to minimize the outline of my breasts, but his eyes had already appraised me. Just then, the out-of-breath Captain caught up with him.

Captain Taylor smiled as he spoke. "Morning, Elizabeth. How are you feeling today? Better, I hope."

Gossip had spread fast about Lance's refusal to leave the birthing, but even more embarrassing, now everyone knew that Mrs. Holm had to stitch me *there* to repair my birthing injury. I was thankful that Captain Taylor was being so discreet about the nature of my problem, especially in front of this stranger.

"I'm feeling better now, Captain. Thank you for asking."

I continued to mask my pain with a gracious smile, but the Captain seemed to sense my pain, despite my act.

"I'm mighty glad to hear that. Now, little lady, I want you to meet somebody. This is the man you've been hearing about. Logan Halliday." The Captain grinned proudly. "Logan, this is Elizabeth Maycroft, a fine lady. Prettiest lady on the trail."

The frontiersman stepped forward and took off his hat. When he bowed, he made no attempt to hide the admiration in his eyes, and as he bent forward, a winsome lock of dark hair fell across his forehead. His eyes sparked as they met mine and his face had already spread into an eager smile.

Its passion was echoed in his voice as he spoke to me.

"Powerful nice to meet you, ma'am."

His warm eyes stared without mercy, and when I spoke, my voice was more of a nervous half-whisper.

"I'm very pleased to meet you. I've read so many exciting newspaper reports of your many adventures." I put my hand up to my eyes to shield them from the sun, and, I must admit, to get a better look at him. "You must be a very brave man to have chosen such a dangerous profession, Mr. Halliday."

"You can call me Logan, ma'am. 'Round these parts, everybody does, and I'm about as brave as I have to be." When he grinned at me, his tanned face crinkled from too much sun. "You certainly are a mighty pretty young woman, Elizabeth."

He didn't notice Lance approaching.

"The lady's name is Mrs. Maycroft *and I'm her husband.*" Lance's voice cut the air like a knife.

"Pleased to meet you, Sir. I didn't mean any harm to your lady. It's just that she's so lovely and appealin', sittin' there with the sunlight shinin' on her hair. You're a mighty lucky man, Mr. Maycroft. You sure are!"

A muscle flicked angrily in Lance's jaw and his jealousy showed itself as he shook the frontiersman's hand much harder than necessary. When Lance spoke again, his harsh tone was as rigid as his handshake.

"Just remember that she's a married woman with a newborn baby. This journey is difficult enough without new problems. *Do we understand each other, Mr. Halliday?*"

"Sure, Mr. Maycroft. I didn't mean any harm. I'm just a friendly sort, I guess. Maybe I could help you with somethin' that needs fixin' to make up for any slight I've caused."

But Lance was already shaking his head *no.*

"I'm quite capable, Mr. Halliday. *I don't need your help.*"

"Well, it's powerful nice meetin' you anyway."

Lance didn't answer.

Logan Halliday said a quick farewell to Lance, then he turned to me with a charmingly wicked smile and a wink as he left to join Captain Taylor at the next wagon in the long line.

Lance slumped down beside me, searching my eyes for a feeling he was afraid he'd see there.

He gripped my hand tightly, possessively.

"I can see why he's so fascinated by you, Elizabeth. "

"You know I could never love anyone but you, Lance. *Never.*" I ran my fingertip across the curve of his mouth.

He groaned and wrapped his strong arms around my shoulders, pulling me tightly to him.

"My God, Elizabeth. I want you so desperately, but I'm afraid I might hurt you. The midwife warned me not to touch you . . . not this soon."

"She said nothing about kissing."

I smiled a seductive smile and he groaned again as our lips touched.

His intimate kiss was hungry and full of frustrated passions. It made us crave the joy of our moist bodies thrashing in the darkness, a joining that was forbidden to me, for now.

But a kiss was better than nothing.

Life on the pioneer trail resumed the next day without incident. But every evening, as we sat around the campfire having our evening meal, Logan Halliday was never far away from me. Whenever Lance had to leave, even for only a few moments, he'd come and sit beside me, this rugged, handsome man, talking his sweet talk to me in private whispers.

I couldn't deny the fact that I was attracted to him, but I must guard against liking him too much.

Poor Logan, he seems so lonely.

I feel so sorry for him.

Chapter 7:

IN THE SHADOWS OF ETERNITY

Fragments of a wildfire sunset disappeared under a darkening sky and the stars came out to glitter as the wagon train stopped for the night. It had been a long, dusty day on the trail and as soon as the wagons had been pulled into the familiar circle, the campfire was lit and now, the fire was full and rich, snapping and crackling with glowing reds and golds, fiery colors that reflected in our eyes as Lance and I gazed at each other. After we finished our evening meal, I held our sleeping newborn while Lance and I sat close together.

Our love was like a secret fire that we kept from the rest of the world, but tonight, our eyes passed secret thoughts. Any careful observer could detect messages about our deep sensual hunger and of the hidden desires that craved release. But the baby chose that moment to wake up, stretching his tiny fingers and yawning with quivering, hungry-baby sounds.

The baby needed me.

I touched Lance lightly on the shoulder as I left, and he put his hand lightly on mine.

His slightest touch was still like lightning and had all the fire of his most intimate touching and probing passions.

I lingered for a moment and watched as he lit his English pipe. Blue-gray smoke curled over the classic planes of his face and floated into the night. And as I strolled toward our wagon, the sound of his voice drifted into my heart.

Lance really enjoyed these moments, times when he could unwind from a hard day's work by listening to the trail scouts and mountain men talk of all the days gone by.

Lance's favorite was an old-timer named Zeke.

I remember the day Lance introduced me to him. Zeke stroked his bushy gray beard and grinned as he explained his name to me.

"That's short for Ezekiel, ma'am. It's one o' them good ol' biblical names." When it came to an instinctive knowledge of survival, Zeke knew more than all the others, Lance had said.

Lance's rich voice rode the air from the campfire into our wagon while I nursed his son, who cuddled close to me and made contented-baby sounds, but later, after he was fast asleep in his cradle, a wave of crushing fatigue swept through me.

Fully clothed, I laid down on the bed and closed my burning eyes. Without intending to, I drifted into an exhausted slumber, but I was awakened by a girlish voice calling me.

"Elizabeth." It was Lenore, the teenage expectant mother *(of twins, Mrs. Holm said)* and her shy husband, Eric.

"Lance looks so sad without you, Elizabeth. Wouldn't you like to be with your husband tonight? We'll take care of your baby until morning." Lenore's tone could not be mistaken.

We exchanged knowing glances. Suddenly, my fatigue was gone. "Oh, Lenore, thank you . . . the baby's been fed, and he usually sleeps through the night."

I was happy for the sudden opportunity.

"Don't worry, Elizabeth. Eric and I will take care of Richard until morning. You know that I love your baby as if he were my own." She patted her expanding stomach. "Besides, I need the practice. It won't be long now." Lenore smiled nervously, then wrapped my baby in his fluffy blanket and lifted him into her arms. He didn't even stir. As Eric carried the baby's cradle past me, he blushed when I thanked him, too.

As soon as they were gone, I brushed my long hair until it was shining, then I slipped a cape around my shoulders and hurried outside, into the night of sparkling skies.

And Lance.

Nightfall was clear and gently cool.

A night made for magic . . .

The stars were a million sparkling diamonds in the black night sky, while music provided a cheerful background for pioneer conversations, singing and dancing. Children played their happy childhood games while the adults tried to forget the danger that waited for them further down the trail.

But Lance held my attention now. There he was, sitting quietly by the fire, smoking his pipe and listening to Zeke.

I touched Lance's shoulder lightly.

He turned toward me quickly, then his eyes brightened and the corners of his mouth turned upward in a big smile as he spoke my name.

"Elizabeth . . ."

The sound of that voice and the love in those eyes raced through me like a fiery blaze whipped by the wind, unleashing all of my passions, those fierce desires that have consumed me, slowly dissolving my will with their longing.

Tonight, it was more than I could bear.

My voice was deep with desire as I spoke. "Dance with me," I pleaded, "and hold me close."

And so, under a frontier moon, our frustrated bodies swayed to sweet pioneer music. Lance held me in his arms as he moved with a sensual masculinity. His body brushed against mine *there*, sending tiny shocks through my clothing.

I whispered to him, "Lenore and Eric are taking care of the baby tonight and Ethan will be sleeping outdoors. We'll have the night all to ourselves."

We read each other's thoughts and smiled.

He swallowed hard and pulled me close to him.

I was lost in his arms when I noticed someone waving to us. It was my brother, dancing with his new love, the flirtatious young Annabel. Ethan's eyes, blazing across the space between us, told me that he loved her already.

I smiled and waved to them, then closed my eyes and moved closer to my husband.

Tonight, I belonged only to Lance.

The dancing had given us a public excuse to hold each other close and I savored the sublime ecstasy of his warmth pressed against me. I could feel his desire, as strong as mine. He whispered into my hair, words of his need. The urgency of his words caressed my ears and floated into my heart.

My body was on fire. Only *he* could quench the flames.

Perhaps it was too soon after our baby's birth to think about being together. (Mrs. Holm would have a fit! What if we conceive another baby? Here we are, in the middle of nowhere, with danger and death all around us!) She warned us to control ourselves for a little while longer, insisting that we shouldn't think of having a baby until after we're settled in California. But the only ways to prevent birth were unreliable, inadequate or downright dangerous. She suggested celibacy, but with a love like ours and a marriage so perfect that I'm afraid it can't last, celibacy wasn't the answer.

And so, I told myself that this was a safe time for me. I should have known better, but in Lance's princely presence, I melt like the warm honey that flows from me and all my good intentions disappear.

His breath warmed my cheek as we danced close and I dismissed all practical thoughts, aching only for the joy of his body merging with mine. I could feel him pressed against my long calico skirt. Our upper bodies parted. His eyes captured mine. He smiled when he saw my desire, waiting for him.

Words were never necessary.

We walked the short distance to our wagon, and as we climbed inside, Lance pulled the pucker-ropes, shutting them against the eyes of the curious. Then he slipped his arms around my waist and stood behind me and whispered seductive words into my hair as I lit all of our candles. We didn't realize that the bright candlelight might cast our silhouettes onto the wagon's cover, revealing all that we will do this night in the name of love, and we never dreamed that our passionate outcries would drift out to the campfire where people were gathered. *We didn't notice the sudden silence outside.*

Inside the candlelit wagon, my body simmered on a holding flame as I turned to face him and his mouth took mine hungrily. How I adored his touch and his virile body.

His strong hands locked behind my spine, holding me tight against him. I buried my face in his chest. I could feel his heartbeat throbbing through his clothing and I felt his flesh rise and harden near me *there*. He undressed me quickly with restless, roaming hands, the hands of a man whose passions can't be restrained much longer. Finally, I stood naked before him. He stared longingly at my breasts, high and proud and full of milk. His hands circled their shapely curves and I moaned as he dropped to his knees and his mouth kissed the sensitive pink tip of each breast. A tiny droplet of milk trickled into his mouth, then another. He swallowed hard. I held his head between my hands, allowing him more.

Then the man who had experienced a miracle looked at me with adoring eyes. His voice trembled. "Tonight, my love, I'll give you more pleasure than you've ever known before."

He swept me up into his arms and laid me on our featherbed, pressing his mouth on mine in a searching kiss. Then he tore off his clothes and I watched as his hardened flesh was revealed for my eyes alone.

Reclining seductively in our bed, I awaited him openly. As he joined me there, he brought with him all the passion, skill and creativity that his singular masculinity had given him. He started with my lips, then my flesh weakened as his mouth descended from my face, down my throat, over my rounded breasts and firm stomach to secret places beyond. The honey that flowed from me soon turned to liquid fire and the bliss he created exploded inside of me, *too soon*. I cried out his name in my ecstasy as my body throbbed with each rhythmic pulsation.

When it was over, he raised his head and smiled proudly.

Eagerly, I drew him to me and guided him as he lowered his body onto mine. He hesitated for a moment, afraid he might hurt me, but I eased him into me, through the secret pathway of liquid fire. Cautiously, he moved, slowly at first, then faster and faster, deeper and deeper. *Again*, my body throbbed with the familiar ecstasy. He stopped moving and took a gasping breath, savoring my pleasure as it raced through him.

And when he breathed out, his life's breath flowed into my nostrils, winning my soul as well as my flesh.

His movements turned seductive and he was thrusting himself into me, faster and faster. Again, my back arched as the wondrous throbbing passion coursed through me, *a third time*. As I screamed in my ecstasy, his moans grew louder.

I knew he needed release. I begged him to come to me *now*. Instantly, he filled me to overflowing and his moan was louder than mine as we climaxed together. And afterward, as we rested in each other's arms, passions stirred and revived and we started to love again.

The following morning, there were more people around our wagon than usual, including Logan and the Captain, who were grinning at us in a different way. Curious stares pursued us as we prepared for another long day on the trail. *We realized that everyone had heard us last night,* and when young Lenore brought our baby boy back to us, her twinkling eyes revealed volumes about what she'd heard last night. Even Mrs. Holm came for a quick visit and whispered, "Elizabeth dear, I hope you used some sort of protection. Did you?" I nodded *yes* and lowered my eyes. I didn't dare tell her.

We headed westward again, through majestic canyons stark and still, as life dealt severe blows along the dusty pioneer trail. Our sublime illusions were slowly replaced by stark reality whenever we discovered the sun-bleached bones of dead oxen and horses beside the road, the living flesh torn from their bones by hungry wolves or other predators.

Deserted wagons, silent and empty, stood in mute testimony of all those who had gone before us. Graves of the dead have been dug up and we saw human bones scattered along the trail — dug up by wolves, the old-timers and mountain men said. But fresh water was our main concern.

Water was more precious than gold.

Sometimes, the trail scouts found water that was unfit to drink or bathe in because it had been fouled by animals or dirtied by other means.

Whenever clean water could be found, we'd fill our water casks to brimming full. Humans, as well as animals, would drink as much water as our thirsty bodies would hold. Then we'd bathe the dust from our sunburned skin and continue pushing further down the dangerous trail we chose to follow.

The wagon train always stopped about an hour after sundown. The men would guide the wagons into a nearly-closed circle, then they allowed the animals inside for their protection and the open gap was tightly closed. After everyone settled in, evening meals were prepared, simple food consumed beside the open campfire. We were bone-tired. I had to nurse the baby every few hours and I was always exhausted.

Sleep was usually sweet and deep.

But one night, somewhere in the distance, wolves pointed their snouts toward the night sky and howled, long and loud. The wailing lasted long into the night, and always, drumbeats pounded out their grim warning. *They sounded closer now.*

I shivered and huddled closer to Lance as he lay sleeping, then I reached out to touch the cradle. I've heard unspeakable stories about the clever enemies we face and fear has become my constant companion.

Sleep did not come that night.

Thousands of miles of raw untamed wilderness and mountainous terrain spread out before us like a giant's open hand, seducing us all.

There was no turning back now.

We had made the decision to trade our simple world of gaslight, cobblestone streets and horse-drawn carriages for a rough-hewn existence under a hot western sun.

But our luck began to run out.

Fierce windstorms slashed the open plains with fistfuls of choking dust, halting the wagon train to a dead stop. Then we'd all close our pucker-ropes tightly and covered the lower half of our faces with cloths, even the children and babies, to avoid breathing or swallowing the yellowish dust.

Terrible accidents happened. Inside the hurtling wagons, precious possessions would fall and crash. Wood wheel-spokes fractured at an alarming rate and repairs slowed us down. We wondered *why* we went on, especially when our trail scouts reported seeing bare-chested Indian* men with upraised knives and tomahawks, appearing on the trail in large numbers.

* Currently known as Native Americans

Sometimes, they'd move into our protective circle and try to stampede the horses, but the terrified animals would make loud snorting noises, alerting the men on night-watch.

Occasionally, we'd see a feathered spear driven deep into the dusty road ahead, a clear warning for us to turn back, but fortunately, most imagined dangers were peacefully resolved by trading with friendly tribes of native-born people.

But some discoveries terrified us with their brutal reality.

Like relics of a bygone era, ruts etched into the trail by broad-wheeled wagons pointed the cruel way forward.

Deep gashes remained in the earth, put there long ago by hundreds of settlers' wagons passing this way.

Did they survive?

Or were theirs the bleached human bones we've seen so often beside the trail. *If you listened closely, you could almost hear their faint voices, echoes of pioneers who had achieved their dreams. Or died trying.*

Bloody, scalped corpses littered the haunted landscape.

The bitter stench of blood was everywhere.

Smashed cooking pans and blood-soaked dolls lay mute, their owners dead, captured, or their soft flesh eaten. Vultures followed us, circling in the sky whenever we stopped.

Again and again, Lance and I reached deep down inside of us and pulled our courage to the surface, courage we'll need because of my discovery. I'm going to have another baby.

When she finds out, Mrs. Holm is going to shout so loud at me, they'll hear her all the way back in New York! I can almost hear her now, scolding me and shaking her finger close to my face. "Elizabeth! You should have known better!"

She's right, of course, but the baby's father had a more heartwarming reaction when I told him that evening, while strolling inside our safe circle of wagons. He smiled and held me tight. "What wonderful news," he whispered, but I could hear the worry in his voice and I knew what he was thinking. How would he be able to protect us? Lance was a man among men, but even *he* didn't have superhuman strength.

Just then, a sudden gust of prairie wind sent cold shivers through me. I moved closer to him for warmth and he quickly took off his buckskin jacket and wrapped it around me. It was still warm from his body and his masculine scent clung to it. I wrapped it tighter around me and looked up into his face, then his mouth took mine in a lingering kiss that promised more.

But as we whispered our love to each other and proved it in more intimate ways, a known danger was waiting for us down the trail. As we'd learn too late, a secret meeting was being held at that moment. Captain Taylor decided *not* to tell any of us about the expected attack. He was afraid that our discipline would fail us, making a bad situation worse. But I wish we had known . . .

We will enter hostile territory within the week.

Chapter 8:

DEATHMOON RISING

I was the first to leave my bed on that deadly morning.

My baby's hungry cry awoke us earlier than usual. Lance, groggy with sleep, tried to stay awake to help me, but he was exhausted and I let him sleep. Ethan was deep in sleep too, snoring lightly in his bed at the other end of the wagon. We were all weary. Only the baby is adapting well.

I lifted my infant boy from his cradle and sat in our little rocking chair, then I opened the top of my nightgown and brought him near me. His tiny face glowed with pleasure as he swallowed my sweet milk and his eyes slowly closed in that special nursing-baby-rapture. How I treasured these moments when my baby took new life from me .... the only moments of sanctuary in the midst of danger.

Just then, the wind moaned through the wagon, ruffling Lance's dark hair as he laid in a deep, deep sleep.

As I watched him, a sense of dread filled me, along with an oppressive fear of loss. I shivered with an unwelcome chill and stared at my sleeping husband.

A feeling of unreality flooded my consciousness.

I couldn't take my eyes from him.

If I did, he might cease to exist.

Finally, the baby had taken all the milk he needed.

I suddenly felt a strong desire to step out into the morning for a breath of fresh air and to enjoy the new sunrise. Holding my sleepy baby, I loosened the pucker rope at the wagon's end, making the opening large enough for us and I held my baby carefully as I descended the steps.

Early-morning sunshine streaked a path across the pale blue sky and warmed my face. It felt so good, so comforting. I looked around, but saw no one. My baby and I were alone.

Suddenly, I was aware of movements in the distance.

A dark cloud rolled along the land.

I thought it was a tornado until I heard the angry shouting and fierce screeching. The galloping hoofbeats of countless horses could mean only one thing.

We were under attack.

There was hatred in those sounds.

And death.

I screamed . . .

I screamed long and loud for Lance and Ethan, alerting all the others at the same time. Pioneers, still in night-clothes, spilled from every wagon. Loaded guns in hand, they were ready for what they had sensed was coming.

Lance rushed us back into the wagon, giving me strict instructions not to leave it under any circumstances, and that he'd come back for us. Then my brother grabbed a rifle and hurried outside while Lance loaded the other gun for himself.

Lance watched as I wrapped our baby in several blankets, then I spread a soft quilt on the floor and laid the baby gently in its center. I wrapped him up in the quilt and covered his tiny body with mine.

I looked up at Lance. His eyes were moist and he was looking at me as if he would never see me again. He reached out and touched my hair with a trembling hand.

The look in his eyes made me want to cry.

Then he was gone.

From where I was positioned, I could see many things — things I didn't want to see, things I couldn't bear to see. Indians in war-paint appeared out of nowhere in great numbers. Many long knives flashed in the early-morning sun.

Some of them had rifles. Guns rapid-fired and commands were shouted. Wild shrieking could be heard. Women and children screamed loud and long.

The noise was unbearable.

I could hear the *whooshing* sound of arrows being shot through the air with unbelievable speed, and many of our brave men died bloody deaths in those first sickening moments.

Panic swept over me like a hungry vulture.

I feared for Lance and Ethan and our baby, whose cry had turned into a scream. I slipped my arm under his little body and rocked him, whispering, "Our poor little baby, what kind of terrible world have we brought you into?"

The slaughter outside grew worse.

Suddenly, I heard a young girl's scream — a wailing, tortured scream. I recognized the voice. It was Lenore, running frantically inside the wagon's circle with her arms around her stomach, protecting her unborn twins.

Eric was trying to catch her, but his injured leg slowed him down. He couldn't reach her in time, but he kept shouting.

"Lenore, stop!"

I screamed, "Lenore, get down! Get down!"

But our warnings came too late.

She was hysterical and she couldn't hear anyone.

A flurry of enemy arrows sliced through the gray smoke-filled air and I screamed again to warn her, but Lenore was in their path. Arrows pierced her everywhere.

Arrows sliced through her eyes like butter.

She fell backward onto the hard, dusty ground.

Long arrow-shafts stuck out from her body like obscene things, from her breasts, her arms, her eyes, her face and her swollen stomach, where they had killed her twin babies.

Eric screamed with a pitiful wail.

"Lenore — Oh, God, NO!"

He dropped to his knees beside her dead body and sobbed. He didn't see the arrows coming for him.

I screamed, "Eric! Get down!"

But it was too late. Enemy arrows penetrated the middle of his back, pitching him forward onto Lenore's dead body, driving the sharp arrows deeper into her dead flesh.

My baby and I screamed.

And screamed.

We couldn't stop.

The smell of fresh blood mingled with the bitter stench of gunpowder and I choked with the nausea I felt.

My mind filled with ominous thoughts. Why did we leave civilization — what have we done?

When I looked up again, I didn't want to believe what I saw. Dead bodies were everywhere, covered in red-red blood. Lenore's bloodstained nightgown ruffled in the prairie wind, and for a moment, she looked alive.

The attackers had retreated into the distance, taking the sound of thundering hoofbeats with them as they shouted their victory over us.

Everything was eerily quiet.

We were numb.

Through my tears, everything seemed to be moving in slow-motion as I watched women with little children emerge from the covered wagons.

Men who had fought in the open held smoking rifles in shaky hands as they were reunited with their loved ones.

With non-seeing eyes, survivors walked as if they were in a fog, then they gathered in a group by the dead campfire.

I was so terrified, I couldn't move.

My baby and I were still screaming.

Just then, the faces of Lance and Ethan appeared.

They lifted my weakened body onto the bed, then Lance laid our baby in my arms. He held us and comforted us for a long time, until the baby and I stopped crying.

The orgy of bloodshed was just beginning.

For hours after, the bitter smell of gunpowder mingled with the sickening stench of blood and vomit. But we couldn't leave yet. Bodies of the dead had to be buried before we could leave this dangerous landscape.

Lance and Ethan were the first men to volunteer, because burial during the westward journey had to be quick. Rites were simple, with no gravestones. The nameless dead were wrapped in heavy cloth, then laid under hard-packed earth and heavy rocks to protect them from humans who would dig up dead pioneer bodies for mutilation. *My eyes have seen terrifying mutilations. I cannot even think of them without becoming sick.*

Later, we all mourned as Pastor Wesley prayed over the dead bodies, including young Lenore and Eric, buried with their unborn twins in a single grave.

My teardrops fell on their grave.

From somewhere deep inside of me, I wept .... I wept for us all, then I looked up into the sunrise sky *for God* and gasped at what I saw! Vultures, circling above us.

Wolves were an equally frightening thought. All the old-timers said that nothing had ever stopped the wolves from digging up the dead and tearing the flesh from their bones, no matter how carefully or how deeply they were buried.

Old Zeke scratched his bushy beard and spoke low of all the horrors he remembered in his long life.

Terrible things, terrible things . . .

Zeke's final words shot a bolt of ice through my heart.

"You can bury 'em deep and you can bury 'em well, but you can't hide 'em from the wolves. No, sir-ee, them wolves are smart buggers. They can smell a man's flesh from a mile away. Womenfolk and young 'uns, too. Nobody's safe, no sir-ee."

Zeke lowered his head.

"I need to be alone for a spell." His dazed eyes, leathery skin and hunched-over weariness spoke of too many years and too many terrors as he sauntered away, into his silence.

It was a daring time of death, blood and glory, and acts of courage were a daily occurrence.

Along the way, we navigated thick forests and majestic mountains in our westward migration.

Our government had assured us that we were writing a new chapter in history, but we knew the reality. We risked our lives, the lives of our children, and everything we owned.

Still, this journey was to be the essence of new vision, the dawning of legend and reality, a dangerous adventure requiring bravery of scriptural proportions.

And at journey's end, we'll find a new life.

But we didn't wander aimlessly.

We had our dreams to lead the way.

Isolated attacks on our wagon train continued.

During those terrible struggles, Lance discovered natural leadership qualities and his advice was sought out by everyone, even Captain Taylor, many trail scouts and mountain men.

And I marveled at how strong Lance has become.

When our journey began, his body was lean and thin, but the physical demands of our westward journey had given him a firm muscular body.

Naked to the waist as he repaired our wagon, Lance's sinewy muscles gleamed with sweat in the bright sunlight. Then I would come to him and put my lips on his, kissing the salty sweat from his face and drying his exhaustion with the warmth of our inner fire. I didn't care who watched.

I saw how the other women looked at him. The handsome planes of his face and the sunlight on his muscled flesh had won them over, too, but Lance didn't look at any other woman.

He had eyes for no one but me.

And I've given him a son.

Still, I must admit to a flash of jealousy now and then, even though no other woman could please him the way I do.

My husband flourished under the extreme hardships and dangers that waited for us around every bend in the trail. The enemy would hide until they'd weakened us. Then they'd attack us again and again. But Lance was a clever opponent. He had become an expert rifleman and was insistent that I learn how to shoot well, too. I could hear the dreaded worry in his voice.

"It's a skill you'll need, Elizabeth, especially when we arrive at our final destination. We'll have to defend our family, perhaps every day for the rest of our lives. And don't forget the baby that's coming."

He held my face in his hands and his voice grew firmer.

"Make no mistake, my love, these men mean to kill us. And they've been known to capture children."

His words sent a frozen chill through me. And so, Lance taught me well, and afterward, I helped to defend the caravan from my well-hidden position inside our wagon.

The enemy continued to attack our wagon train with an alarming ferocity. Scalps were routinely sliced from skulls and pioneer flesh was cruelly mutilated.

Blood flowed continually.

The stench of death was everywhere.

Lance and Ethan were wounded many times, and I'd weep as I bandaged their wounds.

They were the bravest of our ever-decreasing numbers and I marveled at their courage. But I worried that I lacked the strength I needed so desperately. Lance sensed my despair and gave me a compassionate solution to my problem.

"Every morning before we leave our bed, my love, look into my eyes. Take strength from me. I will give you all you need." After that, I'd gaze into his face each new day, and like magic, something invisible seemed to pass between us. I grew stronger with a strength I'd need in days to come.

We continued pushing westward for what seemed like an eternity, conquering dusty plains, treacherous mountain passes, swollen rivers and perilous canyons. We fought many hostile enemies, paying with blood, scalps and lives.

And every evening, when the orange sun set behind the mountains, we'd gaze into the campfire and we'd remember the world we left behind on those tender evenings, our only reward after a hard day's travel. Sometimes, Captain Taylor would play his fiddle, Logan would always entertain us with clever tales of his narrow-escapes. The mountain men would tell tall tales of wild adventures in bygone days, and Pastor Wesley's jolly laughter could always push away our fear for a while.

But night always deepened quickly.

Those of us who could, would sleep the sleep of the dead. Those who couldn't would stay awake and worry. Many pioneers were half-crazed from lack of sleep and tempers flared constantly.

The darkness was closing in on us fast.

Day after day, the enemy weakened what little strength we had left, warning us to re-trace the weary miles and return to the life we once knew. But we had no choice, and worse still, we're way behind schedule. Long weeks have turned into months. If an early winter snowstorm blocks the mountain passes, it could result in starvation and death for many of us.

Then one night, something tragic happened.

Chapter 9:

A SILENT SCREAM

Under a sundown moon, our prairie caravan moved slowly toward tonight's resting place.

I smiled at my little baby boy, secure in his cradle. Just then, one of our wagon wheels rolled over a large boulder, half-buried in the ground. The wagon tilted and nearly fell over. I was thrown out of bed and hurled onto the hard wood floor. A fierce pain coiled through my body.

I screamed . . .

Lance bolted into the wagon's dimly-lit interior and lifted me onto our bed while Ethan ran to get the midwife.

After examining me, Mrs. Holm said that my labor had already started. The baby would come quickly now. She also said that we must prepare ourselves for the worst.

Babies always died when born this early.

We'll be stopping for the night soon, but now, I'm lying in my bed, alone with my fear and unprepared for the timeless human drama just hours away. The pains were coming faster and faster. *No*, I thought, *this can't be happening . . .*

With all of Lance's talents, he didn't have the power to postpone a baby's birthing, and Mrs. Holm had nothing in her magic medicine bag to stop labor, once it had started.

Worry hung heavy on the cool night air as the silver-haired midwife moved efficiently, preparing her instruments, stacking clean blankets and giving instructions to her young assistants. Our little boy became frightened by the confusion, and he began to cry. I held him close, but still he cried.

Mrs. Holm comforted me with a grandmotherly smile.

"No need to worry, Elizabeth. We have a highly capable wet-nurse who can take care of your son until your new baby is born." She carried Richard to one of the young midwives.

"Take the boy to Mrs. Tawson, then come back quickly!"

The weather had grown much cooler, almost cold. Lance covered me with blankets to keep me warm in the nighttime chill, then he sat beside me, just as he had for my first birthing.

But this time, it was different.

This time, the women accepted his presence without a fuss, and in the interval between pains, Lance comforted me, reminding me of the passionate night this baby was conceived. He said our love will last forever and he created pretty pictures in my mind about all the happiness to come.

He had already made plans to build a fairytale rocking-horse for our children. He described it in detail, diverting my mind from my pain.

"We'll name him Pegasus, the horse of the myths, whose snow-white wings can fly them to the stars or wherever their imaginations will lead them. We'll tell our children that he escaped from a fantasy carousel, just to belong to them."

Lance's resonant voice lifted me far above my pain and vibrated through my mind, body and soul with its most singular sound. It was like purest honey — warm, sweet and satisfying, making the hours of my second birthing easier.

Before morning, our baby girl was born.

But something was wrong.

Terribly wrong.

Immediately after the birth, Mrs. Holm patted the tiny baby's back, very gently, but our new little girl didn't cry.

She just laid there, silent and limp.

I wiped my tears away, just to see her clearly.

Her mouth was open in a silent scream.

She was the smallest baby I had ever seen.

She looked like a miniature doll, the kind I played with when I was a little girl. Although she was perfectly formed, she looked somehow *unfinished*. Her flesh was shiny and I could see tiny blue veins through her nearly-transparent skin. Her fingernails were so tiny, they were nearly invisible to me.

Mrs. Holm fought back her tears and patted the baby's back again. Suddenly, the faint fragment of a cry emerged from the baby's tiny mouth. It was barely audible.

It sounded like the cry of a newborn kitten.

Mrs. Holm's chin quivered as she spoke.

"You have a perfect baby girl, Elizabeth. I'll clean her up a bit, then I'll bring her to you. Have you chosen her name? "

My voice broke as I said her name, the name Lance and I had agreed upon when we lived in New York, a lifetime ago, "Purity." With a forced smile, Mrs. Holm took our new baby girl to Ethan's empty bed. As she cleaned the tiny baby, she called out to one of the midwives, but panic colored her words.

"Find Pastor Wesley. Tell him to hurry — and be quick about it!" A grim request spoken with a sharp tongue, it could mean only one thing. Our baby girl was dead, or dying.

When the youngest midwife became hysterical, Mrs. Holm dismissed her immediately. Lance rushed to see what was happening, but the midwife's hushed whispering and the quick tears in Lance's eyes sent me a tragic message.

"Bring my baby to me!" I cried out.

The new father wrapped his tiny baby in warm blankets and laid her in my waiting arms.

Then he knelt by the bed and looked into my eyes, but although he had no words for me, his sorrow showed itself in the hopeless tears that poured down his face like a raging river.

"No, Lance," I screamed. "Oh, please . . . NO!"

I looked down at our new baby.

Her skin was a deathly shade, pale and nearly blue. She was barely alive. I opened her blankets slightly, just enough to look at her. Her tiny chest did not rise and fall with a baby's normal breathing. With my hand, I tried to feel her heartbeat, but I couldn't. Then I laid my ear against her tiny chest, but I only heard a faint heartbeat. It sounded so far away.

Through my tears, I looked down at the new life I held in my arms. Purity had been well-named. Her face looked like a cherub's with long delicate eyelashes and a virtuous innocence shone around her like an aura. I realized that I could not accept her death. *I cannot let this baby die . . .*

NO — I will not abandon my baby here in this desolate wilderness. I will not bury her for the ravenous wolves to dig up and devour or for those who would desecrate her body with mutilation. Her tiny bones will not lay at the side of the trail, bleached white by the burning sun. We didn't bring her into this world to lose her now. I have never been a strong woman, but by God, I will be strong for her. She will not die.

Mrs. Holm leaned over me. "Let me listen to her heart, Elizabeth." Afterward, she closed the blankets over our dying baby until only her tiny face and hands peeked out. Mrs. Holm put her hand on my shoulder. "Elizabeth, she was born much too early. Let her go in peace."

"No," I screamed. "How could you ask me to let her die!" If the baby would take milk from me, she might live. I opened the bodice of my nightgown and held her close to me, but she didn't have enough energy to nurse.

Mrs. Holm pleaded with Lance. "Please, sir, speak to your wife." Her voice grew louder. "Make her understand. It's for the child's own good." But Lance continued to kneel by the bed, silently holding one of his baby's tiny hands, looking at her, memorizing her face. *But he didn't ask me to let her die.*

"I'm not giving up, Lance." I held her close, giving her my own life's warmth. *"I'm not going to let death have her."*

Her breathing was too shallow and frighteningly still. She struggled for each breath with a strength she didn't have. I would somehow give her my own. Softly, with my finger, I stroked her face, then around her mouth, hoping to stimulate her instinct to nurse. Lance watched as I talked softly to her, keeping her tiny mouth within reach of my breast. Then I pressed a droplet of my sweet milk onto her quivering tongue, holding her head up to make it easier for her to swallow.

She swallowed it with difficulty.

Then I gave her a second droplet of rich milk and more stroking around her mouth. Another painful swallow. I sang her a lullaby. I talked softly to her. I told her how much we loved her already. I did anything that might stir her into life.

I had to touch the spirit within her and nurture her instinct for survival.

If I fail, she will die.

Mrs. Holm watched with pity in her eyes. "Let her go, Elizabeth. She'll suffer if she lives. It's nature's way."

My voice broke into sobbing.

"I *can't* let her die. She was conceived in love and, by God, she *will* survive because of that love." I continued to press droplets of milk into my baby girl's mouth, holding her close and willing my life to flow into her frail body.

I wished, I prayed, I begged.

I needed a miracle.

Endless moments passed . . more droplets of sweet milk on my baby's tongue, more stroking around her mouth, more quiet lullabies, more hope rising within me.

At that point, I was acting on instinct alone.

Then a miracle happened.

The baby's mouth moved, *on its own,* toward the source of the sweet milk she had tasted. Fragile and delicate, newborn Purity Maycroft began to nurse.

"She's going to live!" I shouted.

Lance was silent, but his eyes looked at me with the awe and worship I'd seen there so many times before. He held the baby and I close within the circle of his arms while the tiny fragile baby took her first nourishment from me.

He whispered into my hair.

"You've done it, my love! You've saved her!"

Mrs. Holm smiled through her tears and whispered to Lance. "I'll be just outside. Call me when the baby has finished nursing. There's more to be done for your new baby, and I must attend to Elizabeth's medical needs. "

She leaned close to Lance. *"Remember last time."*

Our new little girl has the delicacy of a baby bird. Mrs. Holm feels that Purity's major problem is a weakness in her heart, *an undeveloped heart, she said.* So, Lance and I, with Mrs. Holm's help, were extremely protective of the new baby.

If love alone would keep our baby girl alive, then she would survive and become the healthy child she was meant to be. Her soft sweetness quickly endeared her to everyone, and soon, she became the darling of the entire wagon train.

Shortly after the new baby's birth, Pastor Wesley's family came for a visit. They brought little presents and he christened her privately. Captain Taylor's wife made a cuddly toy for the baby, and Logan stopped by with presents for both of us.

Logan's gift to me was a big cluster of vivid wildflowers that he'd gathered from a sleepy meadow just off the trail. The baby's gift was all wrapped up in pretty ribbons, tied with Mrs. Holm's trademark bows. Inside, we found a small stuffed teddy bear the same color as Logan's jacket. *As he left us, we noticed that a small piece on the lower back part of his jacket was missing.* My heart overflowed with gratitude and I called to him, but he was gone. I'll thank him later, in my own way.

Logan continued to be good to us as a deep friendship grew, and the new baby continued to be surrounded by love.

Our son, still a baby himself, loved his new little sister. He'd watch her for hours on end. Ethan (my brother and her proud new uncle) adored his tiny new niece as much as he loved our first baby, Richard. Mrs. Holm fell in love with her, too, constantly cuddling her and bringing handmade gifts, most of them soft little dolls for her to play with.

I was especially thankful for all the warm extra-small baby clothes, sewn by grandmotherly hands . . . *healing hands.*

The greatest danger to our new infant was the jolting of the wagon's wheels. Whenever the wagon was moving, one of us would hold her safely in our arms, resting on soft pillows to cushion her fragile body. Each day, she grew stronger. She was our own personal angel as our dangerous journey continued.

New dangers surrounded us, daring us at every turn, and nature was providing difficulties, too.

Fortunately, Captain Taylor, as well as all the trail scouts and map makers, hired hands, mountain men and professional hunters, were resourceful experts, experienced in the unique hardships found on the pioneer trail.

They had skills and an instinctive intelligence that could find a solution for every obstacle that blocked the trail and stood between us and our destination. Every modest incline, every entry into a deep valley or up a steep mountain foothill, needed their sharp minds and expert hands.

Using heavy ropes, they would maneuver wagons and animals up, down or around all obstructions. Their abilities and vast knowledge kept us in awe. We couldn't have survived without those brave men.

Crossing a river was one of their most impressive feats. They'd remove the wagon-wheels, and if the wagon was well-caulked, it floated like a ship that could be reassembled on the other side. But not even these accomplished men could out-guess nature. Sometimes, in trying to cross a river, we'd encounter rapids that meant danger or death.

Many wagons were dashed onto sharp rocks, splintered and destroyed, carried away by the onrushing flood. Precious heirlooms were lost to a watery tomb and many families turned back in despair. *We hope they made it.* As for us, we had come too far now to turn back and we consciously chose to accept whatever challenges awaited us.

But there were other dangers. Like a grim pathfinder, cholera had stalked us across the land, claiming even more lives on our westward migration than it had in the crowded cities, pointing out its victims with a cold efficiency and fingers made of ice. Death was certain. This was a horror that no victim survived and we all kept watch for the fatal symptoms. It seemed odd, somehow . . . many of us were dying from the very things we'd sought to escape in the east. We thought we were safe from the epidemics.

We were wrong, and impossible obstacles continued to plague us. After each descent down a steep slope, the overland expedition was forced to stop and repair the wagons or their undercarriages, which creaked worse with each new day on the trail. Axles constantly needed lubrication and repair.

And every night, our wagons were moved into the familiar circle. Captain Taylor scheduled night-watches, with several men guarding on each shift.

We had much to dread.

There were invisible dangers, those created by man and disasters created by nature's whims.

We were forced to push on harder and faster, to make up for all the time we'd lost in too many delays. One by one, as people found the paradise they had been seeking or were just too tired to go on, wagons dropped out of the long line.

Soon there were only a few wagons left, including ours.

Lance, Ethan, Richard, Purity and I, all pushed ourselves well past our human limits.

But Lance was our strength and our courage.

It was his faith that kept us going in our vulnerable little group of covered wagons, including the one carrying flirtatious Annabel and her doting parents. Annabel's mother and father have already decided to settle near us, most likely because of the growing romance between Annabel and my brother.

Although new obstacles halted us, it was Lance's belief in us *and in our dream* that kept us going. He kept reminding us of all that we'd been through and how we had met dangerous perils with a courage we didn't realize we had, until it had been tested. It was this courage, he assured us, that would see us through these final days of our ordeal.

"Elizabeth," he pleaded. "Don't forget our dream."

He put one arm around me, then gently raised my chin with his other hand so that my eyes were looking up at the nighttime sky.

The stars glittered like diamonds on black velvet.

"Look at the stars, Elizabeth. They'll guide us. I promised you a wonderful life and I'll keep that promise."

He hugged me tightly and whispered, "I will . . ."

Even in the worst of circumstances, the love we shared was like a mysterious flame that the rest of the world couldn't see. Like an heirloom treasure, it was ours alone. From the first moment we met, we had gazed into each other's eyes, but now, our eyes were turned toward the western sunset and the future.

He savored my waiting mouth with his, searching for my exhausted inner strength, trying to give me some of his own. The touch of his hand on mine was like a shaft of lightning, and whenever I was in his arms, I was safe from all harm.

But somewhere in the distance, a tribal drum beat out its deadly warning.

My heart jumped at the sound.

He sensed my fear and searched deep into my eyes, past all the fear and worry he saw there, then he covered my mouth with a lingering kiss.

My flesh warmed quickly to his touch and my feminine body invited him to come in and explore its softness. His body had already answered my siren call, and our fear melted into passion as we lost ourselves in each other.

Chapter 10:

EMERALD EDENS, DIAMOND STARS

Our food supplies were dwindling.

We were always thirsty.

The babies were weak.

We had to take many detours to find food, and especially, water. Our bodies were always parched and our mouths were always dry.

A constant layer of yellowish dust covered our skin.

Whenever we'd find clean water, we'd all bathe, then fill our water casks way up to the top until they were spilling over. It was precious to us, more precious than waking up tomorrow.

Life seemed to be slipping through our fingers and there was nothing we could do to stop it.

Desperately close to the end of our endurance, we had met every hardship brought forth by man and nature. So far, we had survived. But the cost in human misery was high and this last part of our journey was, by far, the most deadly.

If only we could find *home* . . .

It had called to us with a seductive song and we were held captive by its elusive promises.

Its voice grew louder as we grew weaker.

It had rained heavily during the past several hours, but now the sun was shining.

I could smell the sweet scent of cool meadow grass.

Our wagon had been creaking badly, and if we expected to go any further, the undercarriage had to be repaired.

But our fears mingled with the real possibility of being stranded in hostile territory. We would be isolated and alone.

Lance and Ethan decided to make an unscheduled detour to do the repairs, and Annabel's parents followed us to make minor repairs of their own. After notifying the Captain and Annabel's mother and father, Lance led the oxen up a small hill, then I felt the wagon become level again.

Suddenly, I heard Lance calling me.

"Elizabeth! Come quickly!"

I hadn't seen Lance this happy for weeks. He grinned as he lifted me down from the wagon. Then he asked Ethan to take care of the babies and he grabbed my hand, leading me over the top of the hill. An emerald vista spread out before my eyes and my breath caught in my throat.

"This is the dream I promised you, my love."

There, at the top of the hill, the land leveled off to the most lavishly breathtaking expanse of color I've ever seen.

A vast wildflower meadow extended into a dense green forest packed thickly with tall trees. In the distance, tips of snow-capped mountains reached into an endless blue sky.

We've finally found *sanctuary*.

Bountiful land stretched out like a gentle giant's hand. The earth was alive, throbbing with the heartbeat of nature, welcoming us with its emerald-green beauty.

Birds of every color flew freely above our heads and the meadow shimmered with masses of wildflowers that scented the air with their sweet fragrance.

Nature's perfection surrounded and comforted us with a flawless beauty. The land surpassed the peaceful picture we had held in our minds for so many months.

We had found our dream.

I threw my arms around Lance and held him tight. He nestled his face in my hair and I could feel his warm breath on my cheek as he said what we were both thinking.

"This is it, Elizabeth. We've finally found our oasis in the wilderness." He took me into the passionate warmth of his kiss, then took me by the hand.

"Let's tell the others!"

We ran back to the wagon with an energy we thought we'd lost. Annabel's parents volunteered to watch our wagon while Lance carried his little boy and I held our new baby in my arms. When we told Ethan, he grabbed Annabel's hand and they walked quickly in the direction we pointed. Then we all shared the bliss, gazing at a new paradise.

Everyone had a different reaction. The babies stared with wide-eyed wonder, overwhelmed by it all. Ethan silently smiled, speechless and unable to take his eyes off the view.

Ethan, our solid rock, our sensible voice of reason, nodded *yes*, then he started walking back to the wagon, talking as he went. "We'd better start the settling-in tasks, Lance. I'll secure the wagon wheels and unyoke the oxen. Why don't you find some fresh water, but don't forget to take one of the rifles. This is still unfamiliar territory." They both agreed.

Annabel was so excited that she let a secret slip. Ethan has asked her to marry him and she said *yes*. She hoped I'd be happy for them, and when I told her I was, she kissed me on the cheek and skipped ahead, slipping her hand into Ethan's.

Lance and I walked back together, whispering words for us alone. But when we returned, a surprise was waiting for us.

A rider on horseback, holding a rifle.

It was Logan Halliday.

"Everythin' all right, folks? I noticed you were gone and I decided to ride out to make sure you're all right. Don't want anythin' to happen to you."

Logan smiled that charmingly crooked smile of his.

"Guess I won't be needin' this." He slid his rifle into the long holster on his well-worn saddle and dismounted. "You folks look mighty happy. Got some good news for me?" Just then, a grin spread across his rugged face and his squinting eyes gleamed with a new thought. "I'll bet I know! You're havin' another baby, Elizabeth. That's it, isn't it?" He glanced at Lance and grinned again.

"Lance, you sly rascal!"

Lance tried to ignore the foolish embarrassment he felt.

"We finally found what we've been looking for, Logan. We're going to settle here and farm the land."

"That's mighty good news! I'd be proud to help you build your homestead and I'll help you with your barn, too."

Logan smiled at me and started to say something.

Lance interrupted him.

"I thought you were going further west this time."

Logan took off his hat and shook trail-dust from its brim.

"A man can change his mind, can't he? Maybe I'll settle a little further down the trail, that way . . . likely on the other side of that hill." He pointed westward, then his face eased into a mischievous smile and he tried to look into my eyes. Although I was laughing quietly, my cheeks blushed scarlet as I avoided his relentless gaze . . . *it had almost become a game.*

I could hear the grin in Logan's voice as he spoke to Lance. "I just wish all womenfolk were as sweet and pretty as Elizabeth. Just look at her, Lance. Isn't she the prettiest woman you ever saw in your whole life?"

Lance's voice was cold and sarcastic.

"Yes, she is, and we both know I'm the luckiest man in the world, but I don't have the time to stand around and talk. I have to find a water source, so if you'll excuse me . . ." Lance walked away from Logan, put his arm around me and spoke loudly. "Come, my love. I want you to walk the land with me."

Lance's jealousy was still alive, just under the surface.

Logan mounted his horse. "I'll be back in a week or so, folks. I'd be proud to help in the buildin' of your homestead." Then with a wave, he pulled hard on his horse's reins. The horse spun around and galloped away, back to the pioneer trail.

I could hear Ethan whistling cheerfully as he put the oxen on tether ropes so they could graze until their stomachs were full. Then he offered to watch the children while we searched for clear, unpolluted water. But Ethan's worried voice quickly called out. "Lance! Better take a couple of loaded rifles. You don't know what you'll find out there."

Ethan tossed two rifles and Lance caught them both in mid-air. Then he picked up one of the large water-casks.

In the peaceful hour that followed, Lance and I strolled the land and explored in wonder and reverence. Deep breaths of pure air soothed our parched lungs, and soon, we found fresh water sparkling like finest crystal in the sunlight.

It looked clean and pure, but as usual, Lance took a man's risk, tasting the water first to make sure it was fit to drink. When he said that it was as clean as it appeared, we both quenched our thirst with the magic elixir of life, then we filled the water-cask to brimming-full.

Twilight was surrendering to a red-fire sunset while we wandered back to the wagon. Along the way, we talked about all our sacrifices and struggles on this most perilous journey of our lives, and of the wondrous miracle of accidentally finding this paradise on earth. Or *was* it an accident?

Suddenly, something struck terror into my heart!

High on a hill, a lone figure on horseback stared down at us. Bare-chested and wearing a feathered headdress, he held a spear in one hand as he watched us.

Lance stepped in front of me.

"Stay absolutely still, Elizabeth," Lance whispered as he lowered the water cask to the ground. Then he held both rifles *point-down* in his right hand.

Lance's message was clear.

He was armed, but wouldn't shoot unless we were attacked. I knew Lance's predicament. Any gesture we would consider friendly might be seen as hostile and misinterpreted by the man high on the hill. All Lance could do was to stand still, with rifles held point-down, showing peaceful intentions.

An unbearable silence passed as we waited for a signal. Was he friend or enemy? *He watched. We waited. He was on horseback. We were on foot. We couldn't out-run him.* Lance's calm action was our only option. Lance's free hand still held mine. After several minutes passed, his grip tightened on my fingers and he spoke to me in a whisper.

"Elizabeth — if he attacks us, I want you to run back to the wagon as fast as you can. I'll hold him off. You *must* reach the children. If you understand, grip my hand tighter."

I did and he whispered, "Good girl." But after several long minutes, the lone figure pulled hard on his horse's reins. Both horse and rider disappeared behind the hill. He was gone.

Lance grabbed the water cask. "Come quickly, Elizabeth. There may be more of them behind that hill."

When Ethan saw the panic on our faces, he knew what had happened without any words being spoken.

There was danger here.

Annabel started screaming hysterically, tearing her hair, but her mother managed to quiet her down while I loaded rifles with the men.

After making sure the babies were safe, we waited.

We clutched loaded rifles in trembling hands.

My heart pounded as I waited for them to come. We had already decided to face whatever destiny awaited us and to accept whatever happened. But could destiny be this cruel?

Would we die here? *Now?* Would our blood, and the blood of our children, be spilled in the first precious moments of finding our dream?

We waited, prisoners of our own thoughts.

But terror didn't come that day.

We could breathe again.

Lance promised me a perfect life, and a perfect life it was, overflowing with sunny days and starry nights.

And true to his word, Lance built a rocking-horse for his babies, with loving care and an actor's flair. The final result was the most beautiful fantasy creature on earth.

He named it Pegasus and gave it wings.

With full hearts and thankful prayers, we built a new life under a golden western sun. No longer would we have to live in our tattered covered wagon, our home on wheels for so many grueling months. It was faded, damaged and worn, *like us,* testament to our prolonged ordeal in crossing this land.

Lance, Ethan and I are no longer the same people we were when we started this journey, for the carnage and tragedy have lingered with us. The fear we thought we'd left behind in the East shadows every moment, but the babies seem blissfully unaware of the dangers and they watched with me, eyes bright and fascinated, as our new home was being completed.

One by one, each timber was hoisted into place. When the mid-point was reached, the men placed angled wood braces against the house, then the higher tiers were guided into place by heavy ropes and the strength of all the good pioneer men who helped us, including Logan, who brought us wonderful news, the promise of a lasting peace with the native people.

And so, our work went on.

A great part of each day was devoted to planting food crops, some for our own table, the rest for trading. And while we worked hard, our babies played together under a bountiful sun. Even though baby Richard (*now called Lion-heart by his proud father*) was barely at the walking stage, he wanted to help the men with the sowing, so they let him scatter tiny seeds into the furrows they made in the fertile soil. Actually, the little boy slowed them down, but they didn't have the heart to say no.

Our new home grew, tier by tier, higher and higher, until my neck ached with the watching of its rise. It was just a simple homestead made of rough-hewn logs, but to me it was as sublime as a fairytale castle right out of a child's storybook, a place where dreams could be born and fulfilled, complete with a fantasy rocking-horse that will fly our children to the stars on the wings of imagination. As the men added the final touches to the roof, I felt faint. After having two babies, I was experienced enough to know why.

When all the others were asleep that night, I told my husband. He smiled and we danced under the watchful ivory moon, while we celebrated another jewel in Lance's dynasty in the ways we loved best.

Our love for each other continued to flourish, despite the dangers all around us .... it was the sweetest medicine in the world. All my days and all my nights belonged to Lance. His face would be the first thing I'd see each day, but sometimes, loud gunshots and the smoky odor of burning timber would awaken me first, signs of another attack nearby. We'd hide the children, then prepare to defend ourselves and our children.

Isolated attacks come and go, and we survive as best we can. All of us carry the disfiguring scars of vicious attacks, *but the scars we can't see are the worst of all, for they destroy our souls.* Several times, they've set our house on fire, with all of us inside. As soon as we'd rebuild, they'd attack again.

But still we go on . . . living each day as if it's our last.

*   *   *

A few years have passed. Dangerous years, happy years.

The love that Lance and I share has produced three more children. Now, there are five — three fine sons and two sweet daughters, crown jewels in Lance's own private dynasty. After Richard (*Lion-Heart*) and fragile Purity were born on the way west, Anne came into our lives. She's sweetness itself. Charles worships Lance and tries very hard to be just like him. A few months ago, I delivered James, our last baby, myself. *Lance came home to quite a surprise that day*, and now he calls me "bountiful lady" for what he calls my "impressive fertility."

They're all wonderful children, most of them healthy, but Purity remained frail and smaller than other children her age. We did everything that might please her, happy things that gave her a better life, such as moving her little bed next to the window, so she could watch the men building our new barn.

She adored all the animals, especially the yearling, so we let her choose a name for the frisky young horse. She spent many hours searching for the perfect name, and finally named him *Mr. Halliday*, for Logan, who's like part of the family now.

Then one day, Mrs. Holm brought us good news.

A doctor has settled nearby and she's made arrangements for him to see our little girl. Within days, he came to examine her and afterwards, he asked Lance and I to step outside with him. He seemed disturbed as he placed his eyeglasses in his pocket in an exacting way. He avoided looking directly at us.

"I believe in coming straight to the point. Your daughter's situation is very grave indeed. You must treat her as if every day is her last. She could die at any moment. Her heartbeat is very weak and it's a miracle she's lived this long."

He looked into the distance and continued.

"As she grows, her heart won't be able to withstand the new demands of her growing body. She may live for a few months, perhaps a year. If you're lucky, maybe two years. But it's doubtful that she'll live past the age of six."

Everything went black as I collapsed into Lance's arms.

When I regained consciousness, I was on the porch floor and the doctor was holding a bottle of smelling-salts under my nose. I pushed the bottle away. The fog in my head cleared slowly. I felt dead inside. My tears came hard and fast. Lance continued to speak with the doctor in hushed tones.

When Lance paid him, I heard the doctor say, "I'm sorry, Mr. Maycroft. There's nothing I can do."

As if in a trance, Lance stood there, watching the doctor's buckboard rattle off into the distance.

Then he slumped down beside me.

"My God, Elizabeth. She's so young . . ."

"It's my fault," I sobbed. "The night she came, I forced her to live when it would have been easier for her to die."

"Elizabeth, don't ever blame yourself . . ."

He held me in his arms and I could feel his pain.

I stared at the ground. "What will we do now? "

"You and I have to be the greatest actor and actress in the world. We're going to put on brave faces and when we go back into the house, we must never let our sweet little girl know how ill she really is. We should tell Ethan, Logan and Mrs. Holm, but it's unwise to tell our other children. They won't be able to hide their grief. It's up to you and I to give our little girl hope."

We held each other and cried until there were no tears left, then we splashed our faces with cool water from the old rain-barrel. With false smiles on our faces, we walked back into our home, and there she was, our little girl, reaching her arms out for us. I started to shake with my tears, but Lance's unseen grip on my arm reminded me that we had to be strong, for her. I held our little girl's frail body and sang her a lullaby.

She never knew.

She continued to be the center of our attention. We kept her warm, quiet and well-fed, with extra helpings of love and laughter. A sweet, gentle child, she adapted well to her severe limitations and seemed content to play quietly with her dolls or to watch me make our family's candles. But most of all, she loved it when I brushed her hair every night before bedtime.

One evening, after I finished brushing her soft angel-hair, I began brushing my own hair while I sat on a chair near her bed. Lance was telling her a fairytale, as he did every evening.

Suddenly, she weakly tugged on his sleeve. He leaned closer to her, then he smiled and kissed her on the forehead.

"Our little matchmaker wants me to brush your hair again." As he took the hairbrush from me, the meeting of our hands was like fire touching fire.

Standing behind me, he drew the brush through great handfuls of cascading waves while our little girl watched us, smiling sweetly. It made her so happy to see us together and to listen to her bedtime prayers, a custom in many pioneer homes.

My sorrow was most difficult to control at those times, because our little girl prayed for everyone but herself. Tears always came quickly then, but moist eyes and a quivering chin were the only visible hints of my sadness. My tears would have to wait until she was asleep. It was so difficult . . .

Everything demanded the sweat of hand-made labor. We were isolated on the pioneer frontier, with no luxuries and only the simplest of farming tools. I made all of our clothes by hand. Often, my fingers would bleed, and Lance would kiss the blood away and lovingly bandage my hands.

Fortunately, the children brought us joy, but only one was truly gifted. Richard has been born with a talent for music, but the boy was impatient with his small hands, so I devised a finger-exercise for the piano to help extend his reach. As his fingers grew, I'd change notes, adding here, subtracting there, like a game. I named it *Our Nocturne* for its dreamy qualities.

Later, the boy added luxurious flourishes to the basic melody, lavish music that would live deep within us both, longer than either of us could have ever imagined.

Richard seemed to sense the inner power he possessed. Confident in his own mastery, the music of great composers held no terrors for him. Each note he played had a celestial shimmer that quickened the heart and soothed the soul. At a very young age, he was composing his own music, entertaining friends and acquaintances with his surprising talent.

Neighbors were already comparing him to Mozart, the European child prodigy, because of Richard's extremely young age and his music's flourishes. Like a crystal-clear view into his heart, his music beguiled, charmed and delighted us with its boyish eagerness, and one sunny hour, he composed a quiet lullaby for his little brothers and sisters. It had a sweet sound, smooth as silk and as soft as a dove's wings. He had created it out of love, especially for his little sister, Purity, whose heart was declining rapidly along with her health. His music pushed away the fear we felt, if only for a little while.

How we longed for a lasting peace . . .

I prayed for it every night.

Although an uneasy truce was maintained between the Indian people and our government, the pact was broken with attacks on many homesteads. But these war-painted faces were extremely young and violent. Their hatred is more vicious now, and the tortures are needlessly cruel.

Lance remained strong and determined, but the children and I trembled whenever we heard drums in the distance.

We wondered if we'd be next.

Happy times were always saddened by news of violence and vicious mutilations. We've lost many good friends, all decent people, to the savage knives. Details of each bloody massacre were always spoken of in choked whispers and a chilling fear crept into our lives with a shadowy darkness. We were mindful of the dangers closing in on us.

I'm frightened for the children. They're so helpless.

When our home was being built, we took the wise advice of Zeke, the elderly mountain man who survived many attacks. His haunted eyes spoke of the terror he felt, even now, so we followed his instructions exactly.

The men built an extra-large root cellar under the house for vegetable storage, but also as a secret hiding place from danger. A trap-door in the floor led to this safe haven, with a special rug attached to its hinged top, disguising it well. Lance and Ethan had dug a long tunnel which led far away, into a well-hidden opening among a thick grove of trees.

Fear walked with us daily, now more than ever before.

Fiery plumes of smoke rising in the distance were always a signal that danger was near, that another family had been tortured, scalped and mutilated with a barbarous rage, and their home reduced to a pile of smoldering cinders.

Danger always approached on silent feet, but our horses always alerted us. Their panic turned into a fearful sound that could freeze my blood cold, and our quiet little goat's terrified bleating was a sure sign that they were closing in on us.

Each of us seized one of the always-loaded rifles, rushed to different windows and waited. And waited. Sometimes they came riding defiantly on horseback, sometimes on foot.

They openly threatened us with bloodstained tomahawks, long spears and upraised knives. Too often, it seemed, we were forced to defend ourselves and our little children.

The distinctive odor of smoky gunfire filled the house constantly and I cursed myself for bringing children into this terrible world. But even if we had to sacrifice our own lives, we all agreed that the children *must* survive, at all costs. We can hear them now, crying in the darkness of the root-cellar.

I suddenly recognized one of the horse-riders. His facial features were sharp and I could see him clearly as he rode toward me with his knife glinting in the sunlight. *The grimace on his war-painted face promised me pain.* I pulled the trigger as he closed in. His horse reared up and spun away sharply. I quickly re-loaded the gun and waited, but the noise had finally merged into the distance, along with the horses and their riders.

This must have been the group of young renegades who have been ambushing settlers, travelers and pioneers caught alone. They are led by the young man who wears such hatred on his face. I will refer to him only as *The Leader*, a rogue and a butcher whose knife has cut down many pioneer lives.

He wanted to be chief of all the tribes and he'd sacrifice anything to achieve it, even his own people.

I will not speak, nor write, his bloodstained name.

Life went on.

My days were spent doing the things I loved best —
nurturing our children and singing lullabies to each one as I
held them in my little rocking chair, which had surprisingly
survived the westward journey.

My other treasure, the large mirror, had miraculously
endured the rigorous journey, but it was shattered by native
gunfire during the latest attack on our isolated homestead.

I cried angry, bitter tears as I picked up the mirror's
fragments. Each one was as sharp as a dagger and reflected
distorted, gruesome images of the dream that was denied to us.

"Elizabeth, don't . . ."

Lance stopped me from my sad duty, leaning over me
and gently circling my waist with his hands. Then he lifted me
up and comforted me as I wept.

Lance knew that vanity wasn't the reason I treasured the
mirror. The mirror had served a more important purpose.

It was my only link to the civilized world we left behind.

"Don't cry, my love. No matter what happens, I'll always
be here. And if you want to see how the world sees you, all you
have to do is look into the mirror of my eyes. You're reflected
there in all your glory."

I dropped the jagged pieces of broken mirror to the floor
and threw my arms around my husband as I continued to weep
for the loss of my civilized world.

Chapter 11:

THE HOURS BEFORE DAWN

"Dance for me . . . please."

How I adored those familiar words, whispered often by Lance after most of the children were asleep. No matter how tired I was, I'd always slip into my ballet costume, secretly proud that it still fit me.

Then I would dance for my husband-lover-friend to the musical artistry of our young son, Richard, who played his romantic piano music with a smile.

But my dance, my command performance, was only for the man I loved so intensely. Lance.

The love of my existence.

The glory of my nights.

If I ever lost him, I would die.

He relaxed in his favorite chair, watching me intimately as rising blue-gray smoke from his pipe drifted past his mouth and floated over the angles of his sunburned face.

The fire in his eyes flashed me a secret message.

How Lance and I treasured those peaceful times, ending in intimate embraces after everyone was asleep.

Passion was always a heartbeat away. At those special times, it was just Elizabeth and Lance, alone in the world. And on those nights, reality was replaced by something better.

But we were rarely alone and we craved the privacy that only nature could provide. Ethan was still living with us and very often, he'd stay up late into the night. When he marries Annabel, that will change, but until then, Lance and I had to seize every moment we could. On a warm night in April, we captured several hours under the watchful moon.

After everyone was asleep, Lance took the quilt from our bed, then left the house, holding hands as we wandered down the winding path to our secret trysting place.

Secluded in a thick grove of trees near a brook, it was an exquisite place, fairly close to the house and barn so we'd hear the animals warn of approaching danger. We knew the risk, but we'd look up at the night sky, illuminated by bright moonlight, and we'd lose our fear in loving each other.

Night whispers promised ecstasy as we slipped out of our clothes. Soon, we were naked, and Lance's muscular body was visible to me. I ached for him and was pleased by the promise in his eyes as he gazed at me. My feminine body, once flawless, was now fertile. It has become womanly and he says it's even more beautiful now . . .

The moonlight wrapped our bodies in a silvery glow.

Naked and enticing, we silently moved into each other's inviting arms. Our hands roamed over each curve of the other's body as we trembled in our passion. Then he took the white ribbon from my hair and he watched as it billowed past my shoulders and cascaded down to my waist.

His fingers wandered sensuously through its softness.

"What splendor," he whispered, his voice much deeper than usual as his long fingers caressed my hair's silken waves, lustrous strands that drifted seductively in the nighttime breeze.

His hands slid onto my bare skin, tracing the rounded outline of my breasts with his strong male hands. He held my hips against his muscled body and I moaned as I felt his hardness touch me *there*. We couldn't wait any longer. He parted my lips. Soon we were submerged in a thunderous climax and we held each other until the throbbing stopped.

Then he eased me down onto the soft quilt, spreading my hair out like a halo around my face. His eyes roamed hungrily over my flesh and my blood turned to liquid fire. My aroused body arched, wanting him, needing him.

He stood tall and proud over my naked body, his legs straddling my hips as I laid there fully exposed and unashamed under his steady stare, watching breathlessly as his potent body responded to his mind's commands.

I reached up and touched him. My lips promised more.

"You enchantress," he smiled. "How you taunt me with your beauty." Then he dropped to his knees.

His searching mouth caressed me in veiled secret places. Profound in my passion, I moaned and my honey flowed as he tasted my body's sweet perfume. It said to him, *come to me, my love*. He raised his body until it covered mine, then my small hands guided him into me. He moaned as he filled me completely. He began to move seductively, slowly at first, then deeper and deeper, harder and harder. My heart beat wildly with every thrust. *Yes*, I cried out, as waves of passion flowed and pulsated between us again. He groaned. With each throb, his life's liquid filled me until I overflowed with him.

Those nights made our lives bearable.

We dared to defy the harsh reality of pioneer life.

Whenever I was with him, the world would slip away and we were brand-new. How I gloried in his endless desire for me. Each time was a willing seduction, and although the fires of passion always burned brightly, Lance and I had an invisible spiritual connection that went far beyond our physical desires.

We created our own legends under a compassionate sky, locked in the celebration of life between us.

Passion would rejoice throughout the night and only the heavens would witness our ecstasy. Then, still moist from the loving, we'd wrap the quilt around us and fall asleep in each other's arms, exhausted. And when the golden light of dawn streaked across the sky above, it would awaken us.

No one ever guessed our secret . . . that the hours before dawn were always the sweetest.

Within weeks of that magic night, the physical signs were clear. I'm going to have another baby at the start of winter.

Although most days were happy, some days revealed an ominous presence, an unspoken terror and warning signs of things to come. But in my joy, I chose to ignore the obvious and planned a special picnic for a sunny day in July, just for the children. I'd prepared a delicious noonday meal for them and we laughed happily as we strolled to the tranquil brook.

The day was the color of a summer peach and the land pulsated with abundant life, a subtle feeling that walked along with us. My two little ladies in pinafores, Anne and Purity, strolled hand-in-hand beside me, carrying their dolls under little parasols, while Richard struggled as he carried our picnic basket, heavily laden with delicious picnic treats. Little-boy Charles ran ahead, filling the countryside with his laughter, and I was at peace as I carried my newest baby in my arms.

Clouds like spun sugar floated lazily across the sky.

They seemed so close we could almost touch them. Birds of every color flew high above us, their feathered bodies silhouetted against a luminous sky the bright blue color of a robin's egg. Soon, in the shade of a tall evergreen tree, I spread a quilt on the cool grass while my children played close by. Just then, little James cried a hungry cry, but he stopped the moment he tasted my sweet milk and his baby eyes closed.

Suddenly, I heard an intruder's sound ... twigs breaking under someone's footsteps ... over there ... in the trees ....

My heart pounded hard.

Then the noise stopped.

Probably an animal, I thought, as I turned my attention to my baby, whose sleepy eyes told me that he was finished and ready for his nap. I covered myself, sat him on my lap and gently patted his back. He burped a loud burp and I laughed as I laid him down on the soft quilt.

I could not have imagined a more perfect life for myself.

I don't know what made me turn around.

I gasped, unable to move.

Stepping out from the nearby cluster of trees, I saw a young Indian woman. A baby was strapped to her back and a small boy with wide dark eyes clutched the skirt of her fringed deerskin dress.

I held my baby close and called to my other children.

As they came quickly, I looked all around, expecting to see the warriors who killed without mercy, but there was no one else. She was alone, and the gentle look on her face told me that she meant no harm to us.

We stood there silently, studying each other. She was a lovely young woman, with skin the color of the sun when it is close to sunset. Her shining hair was the color of the dark night sky, neatly pulled to the back and held there by a leather cord decorated with tiny colorful beads. She wore a feathered band around her forehead and her features were softly pleasing.

She smiled and placed her hand on her chest, saying a word I didn't understand. Assuming it was her name, I did the same, placing my hand on my chest and saying, "Elizabeth."

"E-li-za-beth," she said with a smile that echoed in her tranquil brown eyes. I nodded toward our open picnic basket, gesturing with a clear invitation for her and her children to eat with us. I'd made more than enough food for all of us.

As they joined in our little feast, they smiled and nodded their heads in thanks for the food-gifts I'd offered them. All the children, hers and mine, were quiet and seemingly afraid, but during the following hour, something very sweet happened.

She removed a lovely necklace of bright turquoise beads from around her neck and held them out to me. Her eyes urged me to accept her gift, but when I indicated that there was no need to give me anything, she leaned forward and placed the beads around my neck, very gently.

Then she smiled and so did I as she made me understand that she'd seen me many times before, that she'd been very near our homestead, watching me care for our horses and milk our little goat. And one sunny afternoon, she had even watched me make candles, and the remembrance of Purity's laughter made her smile again. And through the use of gestures, she let me know that she was watching me from the woods as I nursed my baby and it had moved her greatly. But when I patted my stomach and revealed that I was going to have another baby soon, panic flashed across her face, followed by fear.

She spoke fast with words I didn't understand, but one thing was clear. My little family and I were all in some terrible *new* kind of danger. The fear clouding her face told me that *she* was also in danger now, for warning me.

My heart pounded with an unknown dread. The darkness was closing in again, and now, there would be no escape.

She was speaking and gesturing faster and faster, and I learned that she was powerless to stop the horror, whatever it was. All she could do was warn me, and for some grim reason, she chose this day to tell me of the danger.

Suddenly, Lance's voice called out to me from the house. The young woman and her little boy ran into the woods. I called after her, "Please come back . . ." But they were gone.

I never saw her again.

As I started to gather up the picnic basket, the fear that my children had held back for the past few hours suddenly erupted into crying and screaming. They ran as fast as their little legs could carry them toward the comforting sound of their father's voice. Later, they said that when Lance learned what had happened, his face went white and he ordered them to hide in the root cellar, then he grabbed a rifle and left.

He believed that our baby and I were already dead.

But when he found the baby and I by the brook, he whirled me around and held us tight. "Thank God you're all right!" He took our baby from my arms and grabbed my hand. "Leave everything, Elizabeth! *Hurry!* "

With the rifles slung over his shoulder, he carried our baby in one arm and hurried me back into our home, with his other arm protectively around me. Once inside the house, we prepared the rifles, then hid the children in the root cellar, with Richard guarding them.

Outside, Ethan stood guard with three loaded rifles.

In the main part of the house, Lance paced back and forth, like a tiger locked in a cage. His inner turmoil was like a physical entity hanging in the air. Finally, he pulled me close to him, hugging me so tight that I nearly couldn't breathe.

"What would I do if I ever lost you and the children! My God, Elizabeth, you must stay in the house, especially now!"

There would be no more nights under the stars for us.

After the incident, I often thought of the lovely young Indian woman and why she never came back.

I hope she's still alive.

Every day after that, drumbeats in the distance continued to sound out their grim warnings and dark gray smoke-signals swept across the sky with a tormenting frequency.

Horror stories about *The Leader* and his renegades found their way into every neighbor's hushed conversation.

Strong premonitions about impending danger continued to haunt me. I begged Lance and Ethan.

"Please, we *all* have to leave *now*. Something horrible will happen if we stay!" But they both said no.

Lance tried to reassure me.

"We have no choice, Elizabeth. It's too late to go back to New York. We have to stay here. This is our home now." He wrapped me in his arms, whispering, "Don't worry, my love. Everything will be all right, you'll see. Even the Indians are against the renegades. The tribal elders will stop the slaughters and we'll have a lasting peace soon, I promise you."

"But what if . . ." My eyes pleaded with him.

Lance silenced me with a kiss, but it was not his usual passionate kiss, full of fire and desire. No, this was a trembling kiss, a bewildered kiss that betrayed his fear for us and the certain knowledge that we're all in terrible danger.

Each night since then, sleep has been nearly impossible.

When I'd finally fall asleep from sheer fatigue, it was not a normal sleep. No, this was a fitful, suffocating sleep plagued by nightmares of a bloodstained massacre that I dared not think about during daylight hours. I became frightened at the sight of blood, and even a small cut on my finger produced terror, a terror so deep that I couldn't speak of it aloud.

If I did, the nameless terror might come true.

But this terror had a name. *The Leader.*

I couldn't prove what I strongly felt — that soon, our gentle fairytale castle would turn into a slaughterhouse.

Chapter 12:

FIRESTORM — THE HORROR

Summer came late this year, but August surprised us with a cool spell. Before Lance and Ethan left for a hard day's work in the outer fields, Lance's hands felt his baby through my thin summer dress. "We are the genesis of a dynasty, you and I," he whispered as he hugged me, then I watched sadly as he left.

How I loved him . . .

But while the children played and my littlest baby slept in his cradle, I lit a fire for baking the cookies and small cakes my children loved so much. Nearly five months with child, I ached with bone-deep fatigue, but this was a labor of love and I sang dreamily as I worked. Later, I put the plate of warm cookies and fluffy little cakes on the table. Their sweet aroma wafted throughout our homestead and a soft summer breeze fluttered through the open doorway. *Suddenly, the birds stopped singing. An eerie silence hung in the air like a giant black vulture. Behind me, my children were screaming and pointing to the door.* As I whirled around, I saw dozens of young men in war-paint and feathers, bursting through the open door. They were on me instantly and smashed me against the wall, then they pushed something big and foul-smelling into my mouth and strapped it with a leather bond.

Blood trickled from the corners of my mouth.

They surrounded me *and touched me brutally*. My children screamed as the intruders put their hands all over me. One of them grabbed my hair, fingering my curls. He pulled my hair and the young men laughed, but their laughter was mean and hard and brutal, like their touch on my body and their eyes on mine.

Through my tears, I saw them touch my children, defiling my little ones with their huge, rough hands.

I struggled hard against my bonds, but I was as trapped as the children were and I was incapable of saving them.

I cursed myself for not being more vigilant.

My little children cowered in the corner, crying and screaming as they suffered with long sharp knives pressed against their throats. Frail Purity screamed for me. "Mama! Mama!" She clutched at her chest with her small hands and I knew that her heart wouldn't stand the strain. They ignored the baby, who screamed in his cradle so near me, yet so far away. *He screamed loud and long, with a terror he couldn't understand. All he knew was that it was here, in the same room with him.*

Anne and Charles sobbed and clung tightly to each other, but Richard stood boldly in front of the intruders. His childhood bravery only angered them more. They beat him with their big fists and the butts of their knives. Blood flowed red down his small face and stained his shirt. Just then, a menacing figure swaggered through the open door.

This was the face of terror, a face I had seen before.

His grimace turned to a grin when he saw my children, screaming and terrified, and me, helpless, bound tightly. He shouted orders to his followers, pointing to one of the upright timbers that supported the roof. Then he pointed to me and they dragged me to the timber, smashing my body hard against its rough wood, brutally forcing my arms around the back of it.

They bound my wrists too tightly and blood flowed down my trembling fingertips, then one of them hit me in the face and I blacked out.

When I regained consciousness, I had no way of knowing what they'd done to my children, or to me.

I struggled against my bonds again, but it was no use.

Then one of them stood in front of me and said something. Through my tears, his face was blurry.

He grabbed my throat, then squeezed hard. Everything went black again. When the darkness finally lifted, I saw the intruders through bloodstained tears. As their evil faces, war-painted like demons, slowly became visible, I shut my eyes tight, trying to think. Our rifles were under the bed . . .

They hadn't seen the guns — yet, but when they caught me watching them, they huddled in a tight group and muttered among themselves. Then they came toward me and waved their knives in my bloodied face, laughing at my fear and flaunting bloody scalps close to me. All the while, the Leader watched with cold-blooded amusement.

This was the same renegade I saw from my window, the young man who wears such hatred on his face. *The Leader.* He stared hard at me. He was remembering the day I shot at him, the day he led his men to our homestead to kill us all. We were ready for him then.

Now, I'm helpless. He will finally have his revenge.

Inhumanity shone like black coal in his eyes and I saw cruelty in his menacing swagger. He stalked around me in a tight circle, fingering my long hair with his hands, hands that rubbed me rough and hard in secret places where only my husband had touched me. Then he wrapped more leather bonds around my neck, forcing my head even tighter to the upright timber, so hard that I could only take shallow gasps of air.

He muttered something to me and pushed his face into my hair. He pressed his hardening body against mine, biting me. His hands went under my thin summer dress. He ripped my panties off and threw them to his men, then his huge hands rubbed me roughly and penetrated my body. He groaned as he explored my most private parts. *Where once I'd felt only pleasure, now I felt shame. And pain. His fingers entered me, first in the front . . . then in back . . . Oh God . . .* The others watched what he was doing to me, forgetting my hostage children, who could see everything. Suddenly, Richard bolted across the room and lunged at the Leader. He tried to wedge his small, thin body between the Leader and I. In those last moments of his life, the little boy tried to save me.

The Leader plunged his knife deep. Then he twisted the knife up and around, criss-crossing and moving it sharply in all directions. He cut my son to pieces inside. Then, his followers slashed the boy from all sides and Richard's child-blood spread out in a cruel red circle around his body.

But they weren't finished with him . . .

I'll never forget my son's eyes as he died, filled with raw pain and confusion. The Leader yanked the boy's hair up with one hand and slashed his throat with the other, so deep that my little boy was almost beheaded. His head flopped back and dangled there by a thread. They dropped the little boy's limp body to the floor, then kicked it. *NO! This can't be happening!*

They went after Charles next and he died as viciously as Richard had. I couldn't bear to look at the horrors, but they pulled my hair from both sides and forced my eyelids open. They made me watch it happen. Sweet little Anne, so very young, was taken next. They did horrible things to her, terrible things no one must ever speak about. She died a slow, agonizing death, a kind of death she didn't deserve. None of the children deserved what happened to them.

Purity lay deathly still, slumped in a far corner. Mercifully, she was dead, but she didn't escape their rage. They tortured and mutilated her body, as if she were still alive. Only the baby and I had survived, so far.

Then the Leader pointed to the baby.

His followers closed in.

They snatched my youngest baby by his legs, then smashed his head against the wall, again and again and again. They waved his dead body in front of me. His face was a bloody pulp. Then they tossed his little body into the blazing fireplace, where I'd been baking cookies, hours before.

My baby's burning flesh scarred my soul forever.

The bitter smell of my dead children's blood filled the house, piercing my nostrils with a fierce rage that went beyond hatred. One by one, my innocent little children had been killed for sport, in a ruthless frenzy. All the while, the Leader controlled me. His huge hands grasped handfuls of my long hair. He pulled my face to his. He smelled my scent.

My soul resounded with a mother's lament, a muffled cry that heaven itself would not hear.

I was a mute in hell.

At the Leader's orders, they impaled my dead children's bodies on long stakes and propped them up against the wall.

My children's impaled bodies, soaking-wet with their own blood, hung like bloody rag-dolls on rough wooden stakes while my baby's body burned in the fireplace.

My soul was destroyed.

I was frozen in a vast emptiness.

Numb.

Decisions were futile. Escape was impossible.

From firstborn to lastborn, all of my little children were dead. Only the unborn child within me was still alive. I could feel it moving. My tiniest baby's body lay still, blackened and smouldering in the fireplace as the Indians violated the house and everything in it.

They found the rifles and all the ammunition.

All hope was gone.

I drifted off in time and space.

My soul shattered into a million fragments as thunder rattled the air with a roar. My body jumped involuntarily. I painfully raised my eyes, searching for Lance and Ethan, hoping that by some miracle, they were still alive.

The sky turned the day dark.

Descending storm clouds were a deathly leaden-gray and the sun chose to hide.

Summer lightning exploded nearby, striking something. Thunder smashed the muffled stillness and I was only partially aware of a hard rain beating against the roof. My blood flowed wet and sticky, staining my pale skin and melting into the blood of my dead children. The weight of my despairing body pulled me downward, straining against the cruel bonds that held me captive.

Suddenly, I heard the sound of familiar laughter . . . Lance and Ethan, coming back from the fields, unaware of what has happened here. Icy fear stabbed my heart and panic welled up in my throat. *I have to warn them.*

I tried to scream, trying to push the "thing" out of my mouth to warn them before it's too late.

But the murderers had already heard them.

The Leader ran to me and tightened my bonds. With a brutish hand, he pulled me against the timber. His other arm snaked around my waist.

His breath felt like torture on my skin.

The rest of the them hid, waiting. One of them ran behind the open door, ready to ambush my husband and brother.

Lance walked through the door first.

The smile on his face turned to horror as he saw everything at once . . . our dead children, our baby's burning body. And me, bloodied, beaten and bound.

Lance screamed a man's fearsome scream, a sound full of rage and agony. He pulled his knife from his belt and slashed a pathway through the murderers to get to me.

Some of them died in the fires of Lance's fury.

Finally, he reached me.

The Leader moved away quickly.

Lance cut the bonds from my hands, but I still wasn't free. He was cutting my neck bonds when they surrounded him and forcibly dragged him out in front of me. He fought them bravely and well, but he didn't stand a chance. Their knives slashed his beautiful body with a savage, uncontrollable rage. He fought valiantly, but he was finally cut down.

Death came for him slowly, with "*Elizabeth*" on his lips.

Just inside the door, I could see the dead body of my brother, Ethan. His throat had been cut from ear to ear. The Leader muttered his approval as he slashed their clothes.

Then he mutilated their bodies, destroyed their maleness and sliced the scalps from their skulls.

The Leader swaggered toward me, holding their bloody scalps in his hands. He moved close. The look on his war-painted face said that he was going to enjoy killing me.

I have some screaming of my own to do.

Breathless and in torment, a fierce hatred surged in me and showed in my eyes.

I've never known such hatred before.

My anguish was a monster ready to strike.

Just then, I felt the obscene touch of a knife.

The Leader cut my dress up the front until I stood naked and bound before him.

My dress fluttered to the floor.

His eyes were on fire.

He fingered my long hair again, twisting my curls tightly in one hand.

He leaned close and smelled my scent again.

His eyes, those cold eyes, told me everything.

I knew what he wanted.

Terror gripped me by the throat and wouldn't let go.

He muttered to me with guttural sounds as he rubbed the bloody flesh of Lance's and Ethan's scalps all over my breasts and the front of my naked body. I recoiled in horror.

He pressed his hard flesh up against my bare skin.

I tried to pull away, but my bonds kept me a captive, gasping for each breath. He gave the others a menacing command and they quickly obeyed, releasing the bonds from my neck, wrists and waist. As I collapsed to the bloodied floor, they seized me roughly and bound my wrists again.

All strength left my naked body as I laid in my dead family's blood.

I could smell it and I could taste it.

A circular cage of hairy legs surrounded me.

Suddenly, an opening appeared. Another's man's legs swaggered into the obscene circle. It was the Leader. He bent down and grabbed me by my long hair and gave a sharp command to his men.

I knew what was going to happen.

Oh, my God . . .

They pinned me to the floor and spread-eagled my legs. They pulled on each arm. Two of them pressed my head hard against the floor.

Then they pulled my legs wider apart while the Leader prepared to take me. He muttered harshly.

At that terrible moment, he fell on top of me. He forced himself into me like a razor-sharp spear, ripping me open.

Death welled up in my throat as he prolonged the torture, raping me with a sadist's pleasure, gashing and piercing me with slashing pain, scorching pain, pain he enjoyed seeing. His followers muttered to each other as they held me down for him.

The Leader defiled me in ways unknown to me before.

My screams fought to escape and my breath came in shallow, quick gasps through my bloodied nose. His attack was so vicious that I lost consciousness several times.

He took me cruelly again and again on that obscene day that never seemed to end. My shattered mind and tortured body longed for death, that silent sleep where pain does not exist.

Finally, he pulled himself off my bleeding, half-dead body, but the torture continued.

When they were finished with me, their rough hands raised my tortured body against the upright timber. Again, they tightly bound me, then walked away, muttering. Blood gushed from me *there*, drenching my bare legs and spreading out in a bright red circle around me.

The blood of my entire family covered my naked body like an invisible scarlet shroud.

I knew that my unborn baby and I would die and I surrendered to the reality.

They're closing in on me now . . .

It's my turn to die.

Those piercing eyes flashed a message of my grotesque death. The Leader roughly unstrapped the bonds around my mouth and neck.

Then he pulled the "thing" out of my mouth and laughed as he showed it to me.

I realized what it was.

I screamed and screamed for heaven itself to hear me.

All the evil butchery and all of the savage fury on that bloodstained day in my family's history, all of it was embodied in my screams. I cursed them and damned them for what they had done this day.

The horror that would scar my soul throughout eternity burned in my eyes. Then, the moment of final atrocity . . .

The Leader swaggered toward me and pointed his sharp knife. His mouth curled into a deathly grin.

With one swift slash, he sliced my stomach wide open.

The last thing I remember on that day of obscene defilement was my tiny unborn baby, plunging down into the river of blood below me.

It was over.

As I left my body finally, I saw below me an abattoir, a slaughterhouse, seemingly beyond space and time.

Then I crossed over into peace, tranquility and love.

A place filled with stars.

Part 2

THE   SECRET

AWAKENING

The winds of change

bring forth

the sweetest fruit.

A. E. WITTE

Chapter 13:

STARGAZER

THE TIME: Nearly 200 years have passed. It is mid-summer. The day has been sizzling-hot, but now, twilight is surrendering to cool darkness. Random shadows appear and flicker through the trees as residents light their homes, creating miniature islands of brightness throughout the countryside in a futile attempt to push away the approaching darkness.

But the night has taken control. Sunny daylight hours of songbirds and wildflowers have been replaced by nature's nighttime sounds as the forest suddenly comes to life. Tiny firefly-lights twinkle on and off, brightening the dark with their peaceful golden glow. But now, our attention turns toward a charming home set in the forest like a precious jewel.

THE PLACE: A black-velvet sky glittering with stars provides a protective canopy over the forest and the residence we'll be visiting tonight. Within easy reach of one of the world's most glamorous cities, we find the home of a remarkable female, a woman who will uncover a devastating secret within moments. The air-conditioning has been turned off for the evening and sparkling-clean windows are opened to welcome the soft summer night. The soothing romance of a classical guitar wafts through the windows from a distant patio on the other side of the woods.

Nature enters with a whisper and the hint of a breeze floats casually throughout the house. The night is caressingly soft. As we enter this safe haven, we find a satisfying blend of big-city chic and romantic country charm, a refined oasis that accurately reflects the sweetly sophisticated personality of its feminine occupant. We can actually feel the tranquility that exists here, but it's more of a personal retreat from modern-day reality, our violent time when chaos rules with a vengeance and humanity has become an endangered species.

THE WOMAN: At first sight of this alluring female, we get the instant impression that her spirit has never quite settled into her physical body. Serene, ethereal and complex to the core, her interests reveal volumes about her — a deep love of animals and nature's splendor, stirring music, sleek classic cars, dancing (especially ballet,) artistic pursuits, shimmering candlelight, intimate dinner parties, extravagant sand castles lovingly created by the ocean, and her quiet times, which the rest of the world calls meditation. And now, I'll continue to let friends describe her, so you'll know her as others see her.

Profoundly feminine and delicately perfumed, she's vital and vivacious with natural charm, a quick smile and sparkling sense of humor. She possesses a star-quality charisma and a relaxed elegance that's pleasing to the eye and soothing to the soul. Silky blonde hair the color of moonlight cascades around her lovely face, and when she moves, it's with a swan's grace. Her presence is like a lullaby sung in a half-whisper.

Her voice is loving, with crystal clarity and a measured eloquence, and when she speaks to you with that curvaceous mouth of hers, those blue-velvet eyes grant you her complete attention. *She really listens* as she leans toward you in a graceful pose that's both trusting and self-protective at the same time. And when she draws her last sweet breath, there'll be no vicious little memoirs from those who know her.

One handsome man's comment as he watched her dine with friends in an elegant French restaurant: "You can't help but love her .... she's like an angel, all softness and love." He made no attempt to hide his fascination. "But just look at her. Our angel is glamorous tonight."

It's more than mere glamour. It's an elusive X-factor, this fragile vulnerability. Whatever this magnetic force may be, I've seen men, women, children, and even animals, charmed by it.

Though firmly rooted in reality, she wears her soul *on the outside*. Born with the rare spiritual gifts of second sight (the ability to see and predict the future) and the invisible sixth sense known as intuition, she's developed them to a profound level since early childhood. Mystical events are as natural to her as breathing is to us.

She is a mirror of our spiritual state.

People who are selfish, greedy, materialistic, egotistic, mean &/or violent, will see her only as a lovely woman who is unusually kind. But those who have started their search for the truth will easily be able to detect her more luminous qualities.

A starry quality surrounds her like an aura, reflecting her lifelong desire to uncover the universe's hidden secrets and the real reason for our existence, then to share those heavily-veiled truths with the rest of us.

This glamorous mystic has saved many lives, including her own, *and she asks the questions that disturb us all.*

When we meet someone new, why do we sometimes feel great attraction or instant hatred?

How can we understand the misery we see all around us, as well as our own deep depression? Why has violence reached epidemic proportions, and why do murderers walk among us?

Why are we all so different?

Why are each of us born with unique talents, those we'd want to do, *need to do*, even if we weren't paid for doing them?

Why do most children have distinct personalities, almost from the moment of birth? And why do we find our greatest loves and most vicious enemies *within our own families?*

Why do certain periods of history call to us with a strange intimacy, a siren's call we're unable to ignore? Why does the cuisine of some foreign countries taste especially satisfying?

Why are certain new languages pleasurable to the ear and quickly learned, while others take many hours of intense study just to learn the basics?

Why do some of us have a deep fear of death? Why do nightmare visions with leathery bat-wings hover motionless over us at night, invading our consciousness with an unknown horror, a stark kind of terror that leaves us shivering, soaked in cold sweat, waiting desperately for the dawn to come?

Why do some of us see angels?

Why do millions of people die of starvation, even though an abundance of food and medical aid is being sent to them, while the rest of the world struggles to shed excess weight with the latest fad diet?

Why do good people attract failure like a magnet, yet others who are selfish and undeserving seem to have a Midas-touch that turns everything to gold?

Why are modern-day plagues on a terrifying rise with an intensity unsurpassed in this period of earth-history? And why do terrible things happen to some people, but not to others?

Why do some babies die at or before birth, while some people reach the age of a hundred years or more?

Why are there so many cruel injustices in our world?

Is this a terrifying place where helpless human victims are tortured at random, or could there be a hidden purpose to everything that assures us the justice we deserve?

Are our destinies determined by pure chance?

What determines our destiny?

Who determines our destiny?

Why does life seem so unfair?

Who determines our life-span?

What determines our life-span?

Why does "*life*" mean "*pain*". . .

She asks the hard questions of life, questions which seem to have no easy answers . . . questions which have to be asked.

Questions which have to be answered.

Most of us move limply through life in a thick fog of not-knowing and not-caring, chasing shadows that don't exist while our lives spin out of control. We feel like mere puppets with no will of our own and we try to ignore the relentless ticking of the clock, eating our lives away and taking us closer to our last breath. And we wonder *why*.

For most of us, the answers may never come, but still, our questions continue to surface. We must demand our answers *now*, fully realizing that a quest is inevitable, for *quest* is the heart of the word question. Her quest leads to the forest.

When she ponders life's darkest questions, she wanders down the path behind her house and into the lush forest. But this singular forest must be filled with much more than just enchantment, because she's shielded by the profound serenity she finds there. It has become a guaranteed sanctuary and a temporary escape from today's violent realities, a dark time when honesty, privacy and personal safety seem non-existent and human life is all too expendable.

Instinctively, she *knows* that the secrets of life sleep deep in our consciousness, that miracles are our sacred birthright, and it's when we transcend our listless daily lives that we can soar to newer levels of awareness where all things are possible and every wish is granted.

The place called "inner peace."

Her sacred space always extends into the forest.

It's a secret place overflowing with stately oaks and soft firs shaped like narrow pyramids. Spritely spruces exist here, too, along with pink dogwoods, bristly pines, slender white birches that lean toward the earth like graceful ballerinas, and aspen trees, whose fragile leaves tremble in the gentlest breeze.

No earthly eyes watch her as she moves serenely, robed in white, wandering among her beloved trees until she reaches her meditation place, and before she closes her eyes, she gazes at the idyllic view that surrounds and protects her.

When she gazes into the forest, we wonder .... what is she *really* seeing? Sky, trees and songbirds? Or a mysterious realm known only to her, and others like her? We may never know, but if we're fortunate, our desire to *know* will lead us to one who is enlightened, someone who will willingly give us the answers to life's most difficult questions.

Until you find that special someone, *she* can be our own gentle guide, giving each of us a magic lantern to light our way through this darkness of illusion and pain we call *life*.

Because we live in such dangerous and uncertain times, we must allow her to remain sheltered in the protective cloak of anonymity, although some of you may know who she is.

I'll call her by another name, a name she'll choose herself. Her choice is provocative.

It's a name with which she feels "strangely comfortable."

She asks us to call her *Elizabeth*.

The *new* Elizabeth has an honorable goal.

She wants to leave the world a better place than it was on the snowy evening she was born, not for herself, *but for all of us.* And she wants to add a dimension of grace to our swirling blue planet, like a lingering perfume trailing after her as she departs from us and journeys to that place filled with stars.

She's prepared to reveal startling events to you now.

Through your mind's eye and Elizabeth's loving words, you'll see images, stunning visuals of a secret journey, a mystical voyage into the vast unknown with her as our guide. Phantoms of the past will arise with lightning speed as you experience spectacular events. (*Some call them miracles.*)

She will hold nothing back.

Her secrets will be your secrets.

The fascinating, sometimes shocking, details will be told by Elizabeth, for she is the one who has endured all of these miraculous things. But perhaps the truest miracle of all is this. She has survived her ordeal.

It began on that fateful night.

The night her gift turned into a curse.

Chapter 14:

PHANTOM OF THE NIGHT

(Elizabeth is speaking.)

It happened suddenly, like a flash of summer lightning, full of fire and drama, the exciting moment that would change my life forever.

As I was carrying a thick file of papers into my living room, I heard someone calling to me, a man's deep voice, rich, resonant and decidedly British.

Its distinctive sound shattered my calm, drifted into my mind and touched the core of my existence.

"Elizabeth..."

I turned in the direction of the voice so quickly that strands of my long hair caught between my slightly parted lips. The television screen has somehow jumped to life, turned on by something, or someone. *I see him.* The master of the voice was a man I've never seen before — an actor costumed from the pages of history in a televised advertisement for an important upcoming program. As his television image spoke, his words were a blur, but something strange was happening as he shattered my summer night with his proud presence. Forbidden memories, fallen through the cracks of time, were struggling to emerge. Something was awakening ...

A chill climbed into my warm flesh with icy fingers.

My heartbeat raced and roared in my ears.

My throat closed shut and I gasped for breath. A sudden wave of unexplained sorrow whipped my trembling body as my eyes explored his singular masculinity.

My eyes drank him in, then deeper feelings of love and loyalty coursed through me and merged with him.

His voice was like a precious vintage wine, decanted just for me, and each gesture was a secret ceremony, a velvet touch that seductively probed every inch of my body, mind and soul.

No other man's voice had touched me so deeply before.

Like a time-capsule buried in the distant past, bittersweet memories quickly leaped to the surface of my mind as his face continued to appear before me, transparent and floating in mid-air, between me and the television screen.

Gazing at me with adoring eyes, his powerful presence challenged me, compelling my recognition as it penetrated my soul and touched the core of my being.

Just then, five unspoken words forced their message into my consciousness and penetrated my fiercely throbbing heart.

"*Remember me, Elizabeth. Remember me.*"

Although he hadn't spoken them aloud, his words penetrated me like a silent storm. Passion swirled through my mind and body and my flesh was on fire.

A phrase I'd never heard before flashed into my mind .... a prince of a man who named his sons after kings.

Instant recognition wrapped around me like a comforting mist and I drew in a deep breath, releasing it in a deep sigh. I remembered that gaunt, elegant face and I remembered that voice. His powerful presence probed me with strange, far-distant memories of a loved one, long dead. I know him, from another time, from another place. Haunting remembrances were emerging, things I'd never consciously known before tonight . . . antique scenes of a New York City that had ceased to exist since the mid-1800's .... the chilling dangers of the pioneer experience .... and the terrifying day that blood and mass murder swept though a young family's homestead. These things flashed before my eyes, then vanished just as quickly.

My heartbeat raced as I watched him.

Tears burned my eyes and flowed like little rivers down my cheeks. I continued to savor his virile dignity, studying him as he wandered across an elegant theatrical set, proud and regal, with a tall man's long stride. Visibly trembling, I stood silently and absorbed his unique gestures. Although my life was shattering all around me, I was happier than I'd ever been as memories spread like wildfire. I remembered him the way he was then. Except for being more mature now, he hasn't really changed at all. His hair is still sleek and dark as a night without stars. His face reveals intelligent eyes and the finely-sculptured profile I remember so well. His large, expressive hands move slowly and dramatically, just as they did then, and his mouth reveals images that only I can understand.

A coiled power and a daring courage, hidden from all others, were visible to me.

Time could never erase such love and probing passions from my memory, the slender curve of his mouth pressed against mine and the way his man's hands seared my flesh until I craved him more than life itself.

Suddenly, the television screen went blank again.

He was gone.

I closed my burning eyes.

In my soul's depths, it had already been confirmed.

All doubts dissolved.

I have known him before.

I felt weak and I allowed my arms to relax by my sides. My hand loosened their grip on the file of documents I'd been holding and the contents spilled out.

Bright islands of pristine white paper drifted to the carpet and settled at my sandaled feet.

Somehow, through my veil of tears, I found the sofa and collapsed into its soft pillows.

A profound sadness and a terrible sense of loss engulfed me and merged with the powerful magnetism that had flowed from him.

It had drawn me in, deep . . . deep . . . deeper still.

I was submerged in him.

And had lost myself, willingly.

An eternity passed as I laid there on the sofa, curled into a fetal position and sobbing with sorrow as my shattered mind remembered my husband, the way he was *then*.

Endless days and restless nights passed in slow-motion, and at that point, I lived only for the night of his performance. I was experiencing emotions that went soul-deep, driven by an opulent love that sent secret messages to me from my heart.

Finally, the time had come. I watched intensely, listening with an open mind. I barely noticed the others in the cast. Their words and their faces were a blur. All I saw was his face.

And all I heard was his voice, overflowing with a sky full of stars and a haunting resonance, a velvet touch that stirred vague, then sharp, then sharpest memories. It flowed through me like honey with a singular sound that must have come from a mysterious realm. Its deep vibrato reached far down inside of him, and when it emerged, it had transformed into an ethereal other-worldly sound .... rich and resonant, with a smoothness that warmed my soul.

Many details surfaced.

Details that glorified. Details that terrified.

Details from a long-forgotten past.

My past. His past.

Our past . . .

As I watched each performance, his princely presence warmed me with its bittersweet memories and his voice flowed through me like smoothest, sweetest honey. It stimulated long-hidden memories of this gallant man and of the passionate love we once shared so willingly, so openly. The essence of our life together, along with its terrible tragedy, was still within me. But I knew that some details were missing.

I needed to know.

And so, in the enchanted silence of my home and the forested woodland grove, long hours of quiet times unveiled vivid memories. An impenetrable shadow had suddenly been lifted from my mind, and all the unexplained mysteries which have haunted me were finally unveiled. In a sublime vision, I witnessed the first magical meeting between ballerina and actor, those seductive moments that seemed to last forever.

Perhaps they did last forever.

I remembered all the rest with a deep and comforting warmth ... our romantic courtship ... Lance's rich voice reciting poetry and whispering his love for me ... lavish bouquets of fragrant flowers ... a distinguished actor's performances on a stage in old New York ... the sensuous temptations forbidden to us before marriage, so very difficult to control, but we did, conforming to the requirements of the time in which we lived.

We'd saved, preserved and treasured our intense passions until our wedding night, the night the skies parted and the core of the earth melted beneath our firm bodies.

And what young virgin could ever forget a wedding night such as ours, with its sensuous discoveries, its devouring passions and voluptuous memories — how the slightest touch of his hands and his mouth on my flesh would keep the honey flowing — and how perfectly we melted into one another.

Irresistible memories of a frontier existence shattered my reality of today and hurled me into sweet remembrances of all our forgotten yesterdays. I recalled all of it ... the love of our days, the passion of our nights.

It hurts to remember, but oh, how well I remember .... his masculine form pressed into my curvaceous body, his potent virility and his fiery kisses searing me with their hunger and their desire. Sensual images swirled through my mind and my body, with our haunting love at the center of it all.

Years of meditative quiet times have brought me to a high state of proficiency and awareness and it takes only a few moments of totally relaxed concentration. *Then suddenly, inner dimensions shift and I'm surrounded by scenes of a young pioneer woman's life. Elizabeth Maycroft's. Mine . . .*

I'm there, re-living my former life with Lance and our babies. I breathe in the fragrance of wildflowers growing just outside my windows and I can feel the touch of my children's softness as I hold them in my arms.

My happiness is sublime.

It's like a haunting, except that I'm haunting time.

In an instant, I can reach into the pioneer past of nearly 200 years ago and make it mine, make it now. But sometimes, I'm so deeply into it, I'm afraid I won't come back to the present time. I'll be a time-traveler, trapped in the mid-1800's, in a space now filled with lavish homes. But since "time" has (and is) its own dimension with its own subtle mysteries, I can experience it now, just as it was then. And because time is quite fluid and yielding as it penetrates our present, my pioneer existence can exist for me now, just as it did then.

I purposely limit the use of this spiritual gift, because the temptations are great and the dangers are quite real. But there are people who would want to use my powers to their own advantage. I will *never* allow myself to be used by those who would destroy my spiritual gifts simply for their own selfish greed. Fortunately, nature has provided a built-in safety feature. If I am not calm and serene, and if these powers are forced into use by others, *they shut down.*

From sunrise until midnight, my days and nights were a blur. Only Lance's voice existed, echoing in the peaceful stillness of my consciousness. Like a phantom kiss breathing into my spirit, his voice has returned to me from another time, another existence, to melt me with its velvet resonance.

My heart beats in syncopation with its commanding pulse, and his finely-sculptured face mesmerizes me.

His will hypnotizes my will.

And behind his invisible words, I feel his love.

Suddenly, I sense him in the room with me.

"Elizabeth . . ."

I feel him touching me . . . Oh, my God . . .

I am willingly locked in his ghostly embrace.

He surrounds me like a mist . . .

Protecting me . . . possessing me . . .

Gently, he carries me away from the physical world, and I find myself in a multi-dimensional realm full of stars, a wonderfully familiar place.

Suddenly, the past becomes the present.

Or has the present become the past?

Physical reality fades into mist and is replaced by a shared adoration. Our lives are merging, I can feel it. We are one again. Mystical colors dance before my dazzled eyes as together, we defeat the tyranny of time and the grand illusion of life and death.

His presence exalts me and I am reborn, brand-new. His voice whispers to me of wonders to come.

Long-held secrets spill out like purest sugar, prophecies of things in our future, things I must do. He will point the way for me, and I promise to follow wherever he leads me, for I trust him with my life.

When he speaks, it is the creative voice of the universe I hear, a voice full of stars.

I feel soft and warm and loved.

And when he whispers the stars into my hair, it is my own sweet lullaby. My voice returns the stars to him and the stars are love. Together, we are the sanctuary of stars. I am his life, his very last breath. I will always belong to him.

Yes, I am his . . . in life, in death, forever, just like a golden thread weaving throughout the delicate fabric of time and space and eternity . . .

October has whiplashed the air crispy-cold.

In the poignant weeks before the last bronze-toned leaf drifted from towering trees to the earth below, many wondrous facts fell into place. My quiet times of contemplation and meditation have surrendered exciting answers and my heart could hardly contain the joy I felt.

The universe had yielded its secrets like luminous pieces of a cosmic jigsaw puzzle.

Until the wonderful moment I saw my husband's face, my awareness of *the Elizabeth-lifetime* had always been mercifully out-of-focus.

Now those scenes were brightly colored with the blood of my family, in sharp-focus and extreme close-up.

I now know with a spiritually based certainty that this singular man had truly been my beloved husband-lover-friend, from sublime lives lived nearly two centuries ago.

The prince of a man who named his sons after kings has given me the answer to one of my life's unsolvable questions.

Lance has solved my life-long mystery.

As far back as I can remember, I've always expressed my feelings through poetry. At first, it rhymed, so necessary in my earliest years of schooling, but later, as my true individuality flourished, the depth of my words overshadowed any attempt on my part to make them conform to the limits of poetry which had to rhyme. My words suddenly took on a leisurely, flowing quality, not rhyming at all, but much more emotionally rich and passionately unashamed than ever before.

My leather-bound journal, with its pristine ivory pages, always awaited the high-tide of my passion and my impulsive thoughts. My poetic prose has always been a most mystical sanctuary, a ritual, a secret ceremony.

It was a written conversation between my conscious mind and cosmic super-conscious mind, the connecting link between Creation and the fragment of life called "I."

For years, words of deep love and sensual passion poured forth unexpectedly from me, focused through the crystal prism of my consciousness, love poems for a man I adored with a deep hunger, *but who?*

Still, the need was always there to write those love poems, secretly dedicated to a phantom love whose identity has been the most mysterious of all my life's complex questions, until now. At last, it is a mystery solved. *Lance* had been the true inspiration for all the unexplained passion and all of the sensuous feelings that went soul-deep.

The phantom of my poems, the object of my unexplained love and restless passion, was the man I had not yet re-discovered . . . Lance.

How fortunate for the world, and England in particular, that he has chosen to become an actor, for he is a performer whose talent shines with an inborn dignity and natural nobility.

In his twice-chosen profession, he exalts the lives of those he touches. *Still, he has touched no life as deeply as he has touched mine.*

From its embryonic beginnings, our love has had a bright and passionate history, like a skyborn comet spinning through our lives, connecting us with the brilliant colors we find on the other side of life.

Because of him, I am no longer earthbound.

Although we are separated by thousands of miles and a vast ocean, we're alive again, but until now, my consciousness had revealed only the happy times.

A crucial 2nd element was about to show itself.

It would test the boundaries of my courage and abilities, my most deeply-held spiritual beliefs and my ultimate trust in the Creator.

Chapter 15:

NOCTURNE FOR ELIZABETH

Like most of the great moments in life, it happened unexpectedly. At the time, it seemed like an insignificant event, the sound of haunting music, drifting over me like a summer sun-shower. The music's shadowy sound drifted through my ears, floating into the silent archives of my mind and aching heart. I acquired the music quickly, *instinctively*, wondering why something mentioned on the cover seemed so familiar, yet I'd never heard of it before in this lifetime.

In the hours that followed, its whispering tones drifted into the depths of my inner being, endlessly probing, ever so gently. Through sunny days and starry nights, the music surrounded every waking moment.

Like a sentinel standing guard over me, it comforted me, inspired me and spiritually guided me.

Like true magic, every musical note had the shimmer of a gentle spring rainfall. Every melody, a sonic lullaby awakening powerful remembrances in me, embracing and comforting my mind with its amazing softness.

An afterglow interlude of rare beauty.

Sweet as honey from the hive . . .

Music can be as powerful as perfume .... it can unlock hidden memories and soothe both body and soul. The more I listened, the more enchanted I became. Whether delicate or with the rising intensity of a lavish crescendo, his musical transitions were astonishing, a sacred sanctuary one moment, seductive the next, then, as exciting as fireworks exploding all around me. Just as quickly, it transformed itself into a floating cloud moved aloft by an interstellar breeze.

It was like a roller-coaster ride through space.

Familiar melodies were contemporary. Modern melodies came straight from the stratosphere, revealing sweet scenes to me of the distant past, happy children playing in the sunshine and the intimate creativity of an elegant actor. The music provoked even more powerful and seductive memories. It was mysteriously soothing and I played it constantly. But I felt an uneasy sorrow, sensing that the obscure musician's inspiration had somehow come from another plane of existence. I had to know the truth. One night, as I confided to the ivory pages of my journal, Lance's resonant voice came to me, whispering low. *"Remember me, Elizabeth."*

From the very beginning, one of the musician's own compositions disturbed me. *It was Our Nocturne, note for note,* the same finger-exercise that Richard and I kept changing and adapting, together, in a frontier homestead nearly two centuries ago. The music itself would be my star-map to the truth. Was it the music, or was it the musician?

Suddenly, everything became clear.

Intriguing elements embodied *within the music* became obvious, commanding my attention with a boyish intimacy, while recognizable flourishes and rising crescendos revealed the true person behind the music and his well-hidden secrets began to pour forth like a comet hurtling through a starry sky.

Then the music's ideal beauty drifted me into a deeply meditative altered state of being. As I closed my eyes, I waited patiently for ultimate wisdom to reveal everything.

And I began to listen *between the notes*.

I wondered . . . Is he my former son, Richard?*

Years of quiet times have taught me this: It's when we enter the silence that miracles can occur and important answers are given to us. During relaxation and meditation, our stress-ridden bodies have a chance to unwind from the worries and fears that invade our everyday lives. Our breathing slows to a leisurely rhythm and our minds become calm. In this receptive silence, we're free to explore inner feelings, focus on difficult problems or just rest, letting our worries and fears slip away.

We become more relaxed than we've ever been before.

In those tranquil moments, we're in total control of our lives as we quiet our active mind, dismiss our fears, renew our long-lost sense of trust, expand our self-esteem, fill the terrible emptiness inside and ultimately experience the unlimited help that's always available to us. All we have to do is ask.

Richard is not the musician's real name today.

We'll also be developing our survival instincts, as well as intuition, sometimes called the sixth sense. Currently dormant in most of humanity, this wondrous talent and true wealth can unfold and grow, if given the right environment and nurtured whenever possible. Other new powers will emerge from your meditations, including the ability to predict the future.

Best of all, you'll emerge from your quiet times feeling refreshed, eager and stress-free, with a conscious awareness that *you can change your life and face your future with a courage you've never known before.* The positive energy and vitality you carry within can renew your life, heal your relationships and empower you, so you can make all the major decisions in your life with a total confidence. When you unlock your hidden powers, your life can improve, equal to the exact level of your enthusiasm, dedication and willingness. An *inner knowing* will emerge. Your life will stop spinning out of control and the grim bonds of physical existence (pain, tragedy and injustice) will finally lose their hold on you. You'll realize that your mind can change your body. With the natural combination of sheer will, intense emotion and personal empowerment, you can claim victory over your personal life-situation. *You may feel free, for the first time in your life.*

My next step was a drastic one. I had to prepare myself to receive the most intense revelations I've ever attempted, to probe my consciousness, from its subterranean depths to its cosmic heights.

My free will had to be surrendered to a power greater than anything I'd ever known before.

I needed to know about the musician, the third person to enter our mysterious triangle. I had to know the true identity of this man who performs music for the soul, music that would expose all of its secrets. If I yielded to the music, the music must merge with me. That merging would reveal everything.

With only the soft illumination of candlelight, I relaxed in a warm bath, reclining in the perfumed water with my head on a scented pillow and my hair held by a blue satin ribbon.

I quieted my mind for what was to come, then emerged from my bath and wrapped my body in a fluffy white towel, drying my skin with a gentle touch. After slipping into a silk nightgown the color of starlight, I selected the musician's most evocative melody, *Our Nocturne,* the extraordinary one that led me to the man behind the music. I pressed the *Repeat One* button on the music system. It would play for hours.

I glanced at the clock and made a mental note of the time.

After turning off the telephones, I reclined on my sofa and relaxed even further, trying to feel the soft sensation of my body melting into the pillows underneath and all around me.

A few moments later, I entered the totally-natural, altered state of consciousness known as meditation. [True meditation is a state of extreme relaxation and tranquility, a phase of spiritual sensitivity when your spirit becomes receptive and is freed from its physical bondage.]

With total concentration, I calmed my body and cleared my mind even further. I tried not to react to the music, but let the music itself react through me.

Suddenly, I became the *music* and the music became *me*. The man behind the music would now reveal himself, along with his secrets, during the silent moments between the notes.

All stress flowed from me and was replaced by an energetic spiritual force-field, a natural phenomena which appears suddenly with deep focus and pure concentration. Then an awesome inner strength made itself known to me.

I felt a dazzling power rise in me, along with a high level of courage I'd never known before. Luminous colors, found only on the other side of life, danced before my closed eyelids. *Suddenly, a doorway to another dimension opened. It drew me in like a magnet and I yielded to the protection I knew I'd find there. My physical body was growing numb, less real.* My higher self was rising, transforming my earthly energy into pure spiritual awareness. Lance's loving presence was with me, and I was warmed by it as his misty form and eager words accompanied me on my inner journey. The bonds of earthly life slipped away. The musician was here, too, as a young child, a little boy smiling up at me. In that one dazzling instant, I recognized Richard. Lance's lion-hearted son has not yet been reborn, but through his courage, Richard has inspired the colorful ambience of his music, the music that caused this ultimate reunion. For me, it was a homecoming.

My inner voyage had taken me far.

Powerful facts and wondrous remembrances emerged out of that serene quietness, interrupted only by the sound of my heartbeat. Or was it the heartbeat of the universe . . .

Surrounded by the ghostly forms of Lance and the spirit of Richard as the young boy I remembered, secrets continued to flow forth, wanting only to please me with their surprising memories. And all the while, the boy's music surrounded me with its romance and its extraordinary power.

Haunting and triumphant in its scope, his sublime music was the final fulfillment of my most probing questions, from the first wondrous sight of Lance on that warm summer night, until the magical moment I discovered the music that provided such wonders, wonders that led me now to the spiritual place where Richard patiently awaits rebirth.

Perhaps *I'll* give birth to him . . . again.

The clouds of forgetfulness dissolved in the bright light of ultimate truth, but the truth devastated me ... in this lifetime, I had been destined to marry Lance again. Before I knew about Lance, a fine man asked me to marry him. I said *yes*.

At the exact moment I took that fateful step, I sealed my own fate and Lance's. The destined marriage between us was now forbidden. If I met Lance, our remembered love would destroy my current-life marriage.

Richard, our former son, was destined to be born an only-child to Lance and I, during what was to be our current-life marriage, a marriage that would have lasted *more than* a lifetime. But when I married another man before Lance was to come into my life, I destroyed any hope for us. And because a human being's *free will* is never interfered with, our destinies were altered by higher powers.

Why didn't they stop me!

How I wish that the Creator would step in to prevent a critical mistake from happening. [*Free will* is responsible for most of the horrors that people inflict upon each other. It's also a murderer's last refuge.]

It would have been critically important to keep Richard, Lance and I together again. And why had my spiritual powers failed me at that crucial turning-point in my life?

If only I'd known . . .

In their sad eyes, I could see Lance and young Richard contemplating the wonderful life we could have had. In those cosmic moments, I felt my heart break.

Then Lance gently touched my hand.

His eyes told me that we had to leave, then I felt myself being drawn away from the scene.

Our son's white-robed form grew fainter and fainter as we departed from the ethereal planes of existence.

Once more, I had to go back to the physical world, the realm of pain and sorrow and suffering humanity.

Lance escorted me back to my world, then disappeared in a mist, leaving his sorrow to merge with mine.

I carry it with me, even now.

My deep meditation ended, the music and I parted our unity and I was once again fully in the present.

I glanced at the clock.

Only three minutes had passed here.

I'd been in a place where time had disappeared.

As for the music, I can say this with absolute certainty. This *is* the music composed and arranged by my firstborn, Richard, the brave little boy who died such a horrible death on that last day.

The day we all died.

My son's musical soul now flows through a human instrument, an obscure, distrustful caucasian who lives half-a-world away. *Our Nocturne* is prominently displayed by him, and perfectly describes those sublime nights . . . soft candlelit evenings that would begin with Richard's romantic music and my private dance performances for Lance, always ending in his arms under a starry western sky.

When our son is reborn, I hope his new parents will love him and nurture his inborn musical talent, just as Lance and I did so long ago. The boy deserves at least that, and much more.

Since that day of deepest meditation, the boy's musical eloquence has had the power to carry me back in time to pioneer days, where I can re-live those fulfilled days with such superb happiness. And just as the boy's music helps me to go back in time, his music brings me forward into today's world.

What an exceptional odyssey this has been . . .

Through the boy's music and Lance's enduring spiritual love, I've recaptured all the bittersweet memories which have fallen through the cracks of time.

It was through the boy that the revelations came with their sweetly fragrant compassion and gentle touch. Richard's music has created a glittering bridge of stars across the dark centuries between *then* and *now*, bringing us together again.

Time *here* is passing swiftly.

Peak-season fall foliage has burst upon the landscape with a fiery splendor. Maple trees and stately oaks have outdone themselves in their last burst of life before winter's most extravagant frost, the bittersweet reality of an enchanted forest tinged with another kind of death.

Outside my windows, a bronze sun drifts leisurely in the sky, while tawny colors from autumn's palette try valiantly to warm the wind-whipped landscape. The forest's gothic arbor, my sanctuary during the unfolding of my soul's past-life memories, seems richly romantic as most of the trees surrender their brightly-colored leaves to the ground below.

One by one, each leaf falls slowly to the chilled ground, like the soft feathers on a bird's wing. As I watch the scene, I think about my former son, waiting to be reborn.

I can't change the past now . . . I wish I could.

If I'd only known that Lance was a few years away from coming into my future, I never would have married when I did. Because of this, Lance has been kept far away from me for years, and now, our son has to wait patiently for a suitable new birth. This tribute is for our former son . . .

My dearest Richard:

You have warmed my heart and touched the deepest part of my soul through the magic of your musical artistry. Your brilliance is still there in the rhythmic tapestry of your talent, richly woven with the golden threads and precious gems of your other-life childhood. Embodied in your music, you've placed "*Our Nocturne*," waiting so patiently for me to discover its true origin. I detected your distinctive style, favorite and familiar themes, secret flourishes and lavish adornments you once composed as a child of the frontier, nearly two centuries ago.

Long ago, your father and I both called you "Richard, the Lion-Hearted," the English king for whom you were so appropriately named. True, you were brutally butchered while still a child, but you were not alone on that terrible day in our history.

Our entire family followed you in death and joined you in that wondrous place filled with stars. Now, you transmit your genius through a human participant who privately gasps with wonder at the sublime beauty of your music. *Secretly, he knows.*

Your beautiful music has captured my heart *again* and I'll always be grateful to you for putting the finishing touches on a mystical search that began one summer not very long ago, with my first glimpse of your father's elegant face. My inner journey has taken me deep into yesterday's hidden past and will continue for all the tomorrows yet to come. As my former son, you will always have my eternal love.

I hope we'll meet again, *soon.*

Elizabeth

Covered with a blanket of golden-red autumn leaves, the land has become the vivid color of a volcano's fire as nature vigorously proclaims the legacy of autumn's last breath and the dawning of winter's chill. My memories will keep me warm through winter's coldest days. But with that thought, I never suspected that Creation had been protecting me by denying me memories that would crush me with a paralyzing terror.

The paradise I'd found in a pioneer past was not the end of my quest . . .

The cursed part was just beginning.

Chapter 16:

RITUAL FIRES

Days of jet-black darkness have crept their way across my calendar, followed by a relentless spiral of sleepless nights. Premonitions and strong feelings of warning are with me every night and linger near well past sunrise.

Each new day feels like the calm before a storm . . .

In the morning, my bed looks as if lightning has struck during the night and left no one alive. Pillows, unknowingly tossed to the floor during wisps of sleep, float like islands in a white-carpet ocean. Exhausted, I awaken from a disturbed slumber, and catlike, stretch my body into yielding suppleness. Then I slip a turquoise robe over my flowing white nightgown and wander into my kitchen.

Daylight gleams brightly through the sheer curtains and I try to arouse myself into full awakening as I prepare a steaming cup of Darjeeling tea with honey. I watch sleepily as the honey pours slowly from the silver spoon and forms golden swirls in the hot liquid.

Before stirring the tea, I slip the honeyed spoon into my mouth and onto my tongue, savoring its satiny smoothness. Unable to resist, I taste its richness and sweet aroma again. The honey slides down my throat, slowly, deliciously.

Teacup in hand, I quietly step out into the early morning haze, sitting at the table that overlooks the forest and savoring the exotic flavor of my honeyed tea as, with each sip, I breathe in its rich aroma. A mourning dove cries out its lament to the pale-lemon sun that's rising slowly above the horizon and I watch in awe and expectation, as I always do.

The morning gradually glows brighter as the eager sun explores nature's image with gentle fingers and the earth wakes to a new day, coming alive like a beehive in full activity.

The steady drone of early commuter cars in the distance cannot mask the soothing sound of doves and songbirds flying around the bird-feeders hanging from every nearby evergreen tree. Birds of every color are on the wing today, from lively blue-jays to a mated pair of red cardinals, who play hide-and-seek with the sun as they fly.

Often, they fly close, waiting for the extra morsels of food I always scatter on the table, near me. They hop onto the table and my reward for feeding them is to see how beautiful they are, up close.

I whisper to them as they enjoy their morning banquet in absolute safety. They know the sound of my voice by now and they do not fear me. They know this is their safe sanctuary, and so, they allow me to watch their graceful aerial ballets.

Today, some of them are flying like winged acrobats, criss-crossing the sky. I smile at their whimsical natures, so beautiful, so innocent. I'm afraid for them . . .

Suddenly, reality strikes a spiteful blow as I watch a dainty yellow butterfly flutter from flower to flower. A hungry blue-jay appears out of nowhere, and with its beak wide open, swoops in and devours the butterfly before I can blink.

Quick tears overflow my eyes and I have to look away. Sometimes, it's hard for me to understand nature's ways.

My tears drop into the honeyed tea, disappearing into its darkness, and I try to find Lance's reflection in its depths.

A spiral of relentless insomnia has me in its nighttime grip and sunny days have grown dark in my consciousness.

Thoughts of Lance are always tinged with danger and he's in my thoughts constantly. And even though he is most likely in England, *I find myself looking for him in the faces of strangers here.*

I scream a silent scream and will not accept what I've sensed, *what I know*, the certain spiritual knowledge that something terrible is going to happen to him, *soon*.

Even with my powers, I'm powerless to stop it.

More fruitless weeks have crept their way across my calendar while nature has been making artistic changes in the landscape surrounding my home. Towering evergreen trees boast their lush foliage and are still visible in the fast-fading light. The sight of them should cheer me with their perfection. But as I sit here looking out over the lush expanse of evergreen trees, my eyes focus on my journal, laying on the table near my half-eaten dinner. My fingers tremble as I pick up my journal, the habitat of my prose, the place for secret thoughts.

Although my words start out with naiveté, they gradually emerge from my deeper consciousness with dark and shadowy tones. I'm especially sad when I glance at the last page and read aloud what I've just written.

As my words come to life in a quivering voice, a piercing chill skyrockets through my body.

> *"A cruel mirage, this life . . .*
> *The birds will be silent,*
> *the sun will never rise again.*
> *A deathmoon hovers, like a Medusa of the mind.*
> *I move through life,*
> *pale and leaden, seemingly alone.*
> *My 8-X-10-glossy lifestyle shatters,*
> *And the angel in my mirror wants to die."*

I weep as I finish reading my words.

My tears stain the page with my visible heartbreak. A dark mood of deepest blue touches me with its plaintive passion *and I understand why.*

Lance — my reason for living.

My reason for dying.

To find the answers I needed, I had to search within myself, deeper than I had ever gone before. I was prepared to pay whatever price was necessary.

Or so I thought . . .

I wish I hadn't probed quite so deeply.

By November's end, I had traveled through the great silence of the universe and received answers to nearly all of my most heartbreaking questions. Some answers were gratifying and amazing. Others were provocative, tragic in their awesome implications, *for Lance and for our earth as we know it.* But when one wins a cosmic prize such as total enlightenment, one must be prepared to pay the high price-tag attached to it.

The "bills" came in slowly.

Fleeting glimpses of blood-soaked corpses would intrude on my quiet times, flashing across my mind like vivid color slides in a darkened room.

Mercifully, those visions disappeared as quickly as they came, but only for a little while. Then the visions became much more powerful and were accompanied by a frightening intensity. They were no longer confined to my meditative state. Now, they showed themselves brazenly when I was involved in pursuits other than meditation or socializing.

The real horror of that last day on the western frontier, a day of blood, treachery and mass murder, was about to become visible in all its gory details for my eyes alone.

It happened without warning on a near-zero December evening. I was alone in the house, privately performing my nightly grooming ritual in the calm mental and emotional state we all experience when we're doing something out of habit, something not requiring deep concentration.

These are the times when the air seems filled with silver sparkles and the veil is chiffon-thin between the physical world and the vast spiritual dimensions. At those wondrous times, great revelations are allowed to cross over into our sphere of existence, where they charm us with their gentle love and breathtaking secrets. It's when we're alone, and vulnerable to its charms, that the essence within whispers to us and grants us its powerful wisdom. If we are foolish, we turn away from these great opportunities. If we're wise, we allow them to embrace us with their innocence and their soft touch. But at times, terrifying inner truths can descend upon us like waking nightmares, with sharp claws, a deadly ferocity and no escape.

On that icy-cold night in December, I would be forced to pay a high price for discovering my pioneer past-life. Before this night, I'd been spared all the bloodstained details of the atrocities that occurred on that last day, when mass murder swept like a windstorm through our frontier homestead.

But I was not prepared to re-live them. *Suddenly, they came!* Gory, bloodstained pictures moved like a fast-forward color film before me and I collapsed to the floor with all the horrors I saw. My fiery screams released like a volcano's burst.

Tortured screams of my dying babies echoed violently in my ears. Closing my eyes couldn't shut out the horror, the stark-naked truth of all that had happened to my entire family.

I ran into my bedroom and cowered in a far corner, pulling my nightgown tightly around me in a vain attempt at self-protection as my body closed into a fetal position.

I shut my eyes, but the terrors wouldn't go away.

They followed me inside myself.

I was like a time-traveler, trapped in another dimension. Nearly 200 years flashed by in an instant, and I saw — *again* — my screaming young children being tortured, butchered and impaled on stakes like chunks of raw meat exposed to the hot summer air, dead, while their murderers smirked. Richard, then Anne and little Charles, frail Purity dying before it was her turn, and my newest-born baby — *my God, these were things no mother should have to see,* my tiniest baby, dead, his skull crushed, his baby flesh bloody and blackened in the obscene cradle of flames that once was our family's fireplace.

The stench of my murdered children's blood reached for my nostrils across nearly two centuries, and I was forced to live *again* that last day on earth, when even the unborn had died in an unholy ritual of blood-lust and hatred.

Again, I was forced to watch the brave, bloody deaths of my husband and brother, both cruelly murdered, scalped and horribly mutilated after death. I saw everything with eyes that should never see such unspeakable acts. *Twice.*

Suddenly, my flesh began to feel the horrors — *again.*

My body was going backwards through time, taking my consciousness with it.

I was feeling the physical agony of my own slow torture, rape and grisly death in that faraway life. My trembling body felt and experienced the flesh-tearing rapes and the torture that crept through my body with red-hot claws until I was filled with all of its savage rage, its hatred and its fury. The Leader's ghostly form pounded and thrust itself into me and I screamed a scream of the soul, a scream no human ear can hear.

Centuries of hate and loathing swept through me, stained with an intense rage the color of blood. I saw the Leader's vicious face and the faces of the men who held me down for him, spread-eagled and helpless, laying in my dead family's still-warm blood. *I've carried that shroud of blood across the centuries. Invisible and weighing heavily on my spirit, I hadn't even known it was there . . . until tonight.*

My fury couldn't be held back as my body re-lived the horror, that terrible day when hate, cruelty and mass slaughter swept through our frontier homestead. Again, I was forced to experience the Leader's final atrocity and I remembered his cruel laugh as his knife sliced my pregnant stomach open. Searing-hot pain raced through me now. But before I died then, I saw my unborn baby spill out of me, onto the bloodstained floor below, an innocent victim of the horror. I doubled over in remembered agony, clutching my stomach *and screaming.*

My screams echoed throughout the silent house.

I want to die.

I can't live with what I've seen . . .

My heart pounded like a hypnotic drumbeat in my ears as a flood of tears racked and shook my quivering body.

These were things I didn't want to know. Obscene things.

I scream the words. "Please .... take away my powers!"

In this lifetime, the unseen spiritual world of the paranormal had always gifted me with powers that had their basis in love. It was through these extraordinary gifts that I was able to help so many people, to heal and to warn of dangers that could be avoided. Suddenly, my lifelong gifts, my inborn gifts of intuition, ESP, clairvoyance, telepathy, prophecy and the mastery of other spiritual powers — all of these life-enhancing gifts had suddenly turned into a curse. *I had seen too much.* At that moment, I needed Lance to hold me tight, to tell me that everything is all right *now* — that all of us are fine *now.* But he's across a vast ocean, thousands of miles away and I'm desolate without him.

I've been exiled into the middle of a nightmare.

Last night has finally turned into day, and day into evening. A sunset made of red-gold flame disappears under a deepening sky as twilight yields to a cosmic hush. The evening drifts slowly to earth and I watch with misty eyes.

I have not yet recovered from last night's terrors.

My body shivers at the remembrance and my thoughts at such times naturally turn to Lance.

I wonder if he's out there . . .

Searching for his Elizabeth at this moment.

I've been made to understand that if I try to contact him, monumental obstacles will be placed in my path until I give up in despair. This makes me so sad . . .

I pick up my journal to record the latest events, but as I start writing, *something makes me stop.*

Lance is here . . .

Suddenly, a near-invisible being touches my cheek with the softness of a stolen kiss on its warm, subtle breath. The light scent of a distinctive man's scent surrounds me like a nourishing cloud, then I hear him, speaking softly to me.

"I may not find you in time, my love, my sweet Elizabeth, but never forget me. Always keep our love in your heart." He continues to whisper words of adoration, honeyed words that float into my mind, carried on the passion of his most singular voice. His voice trails off as he says the words . . .

"Never was a woman more adored than you."

In a fleeting instant, he is gone.

For the first night in weeks, my sleep was sweet and deep. But as I dreamed beautiful dreams, I *knew* that tomorrow night would bring an even more extraordinary event.

Chapter 17:

A TIME OF MAGIC & MIRACLES

It was a night of mystery, a night of magic. I could feel it, as nature's orange sun disappeared behind tall clusters of stately oak trees, giving birth to narrow shafts of deep, rich light that flickered red and gold through winter-bare branches.

Then the sky turned to deep sapphire-blue and a million stars came out of hiding. Eternity's deepening horizon was just a preview of things to come.

A night-hawk cried.

A shooting star answered.

Suddenly, I sensed Lance's presence, but this time he was much stronger, as if he'd acquired a knight's vigor needed for some extreme challenge. I was also aware of the universe's love, floating above me in the form of brightest light. Lance's phantom embrace surrounded and strengthened me. His face was close to mine and his celestial breath, like a soft summer breeze, caressed my face. His voice was velvet.

"I am here, my love. I will protect you." *Lance, who had promised me the moon and the stars, and gave me a son.*

"Come with me, Elizabeth. Have no fear this night." And with those words, he led me out into the starlight.

The frozen night wind penetrated my sheer nightgown with ease. Sharp and icy-cold against my skin, it felt somehow cleansing. Lance's love enfolded me with its warmth and I knew perfect serenity as we wandered down the path to the place I call *my enchanted forest.*

Surrounded by December's shivering chill and purified by winter's profound embrace, my revelations flowed forth like a raging river, witnessed only by the forest, the moonlight and Lance, whose loving spirit surrounded me constantly, keeping me protected from the cold and other dangers.

I felt closer to the source of all life than ever before.

My senses were suddenly much sharper and somehow *newer.* The thrill of expectation flashed through me while I patiently waited for what was to come.

A new initiation was at hand.

I was ready.

With Lance by my side, I sat on the massive rock where I often meditate and closed my eyes.

As my consciousness drifts to my inner sanctuary, the physical world loses its mastery over me.

Within a moment, my essence gradually disconnects from my body and I am in a place called "NOW."

Time has disappeared.

"I" am no longer my physical body.

"I" am skyborn, floating in endless celestial space and shimmering with the reflection of a billion suns.

The quantum universe covers me with a phantom's cape of stars, setting me free from the bondage of earthly life so that I may behold the glories of the unknown universe. Solar storms play in my hair while cosmic windstorms float my spiritual essence through interstellar space. Luminous planets orbit this sacred space like silent sentinels and watch as this enchanted new being soars through a deep-space sky, scattering stars across space and time with an angel's loving hands.

Suddenly, I realize that my soul is in everything, just as all souls are. I am the breath of life, the mystical song of the soul, a twilight serenade for the cosmos. I am in Nature herself. I nurture on a grand scale, I float on the winds of inner space, I dance among the clouds and celebrate the opulence of life.

Luminous spirits made of light are coming for me.

They lead me to a vast glittering band of radiance, and through telepathic communication alone, they show me how to discover the greatest truths of Creation.

Solutions to great mysteries are willingly revealed and I am shown why repeated reincarnation into successive human forms is inevitable for us to attain the absolute perfection that is our right, our destiny and our obligation.

I recognize one of the winged angels, whose ethereal form floated above my childhood bed every night, bringing me peace. [*The angelic world is humanity's next step upward.*] Now my lifelong abilities are being enhanced even further and new prophecies to happen soon are clearly shown to me.

With new eyes, I see forgotten scenes of our old earth and I marvel at ancient lands we've always thought of as fanciful myths and pretty legends. The most wondrous sight of all is the lost Atlantis. Once a great continent and home to a flourishing civilization, its impressive technological secrets minimize every scientific fact we now know today, for the breathtaking mysteries and secrets of the Atlantean culture now lie buried fathoms-deep under the Atlantic Ocean.

Tragedies in the Bermuda Triangle have been caused by an Atlantean scientific device which, though underwater, is still active, radiating a hypnotic blue light and attracting curious visitors from faraway galaxies in speed-of-light UFOs. When Atlantis rises from the sea with a great heaving roar, tidal waves will encircle the globe. This momentous event will occur in the same time-period as earth's greatest cataclysms, one of which will eventually destroy much of California. Land will also rise in the Pacific Ocean, devastating Japan, Australia and the beautiful Hawaiian Islands, the visible highest mountain peaks of a much earlier civilization than Atlantis.

America's East Coast will experience massive upheavals, ravaging New York and all surrounding areas. Steel bridges will collapse and the once-great city will be isolated and totally vulnerable. Cataclysms will occur around the world for some time to come as nature purges the insults of man. Planet Earth will change and many of us will not survive. But not all prophecies are distressing. The future is as bright as our sun.

Questions from my Elizabeth-lifetime are answered with sweet compassion ..... *The young Indian woman was tortured and killed by her tribe, the day after she warned me of the coming massacre ..... The name of King Henry VIII chilled me because he had me beheaded for producing a daughter when he wanted only sons, heirs to his crown, but my daughter became a Queen.* Other past lives, in more ethereal forms and far-distant regions, are also revealed to me, along with the new knowledge that *Lance and I are twin-souls.* All that's happened through the centuries was a dress-rehearsal for *NOW*, when I'd be faced with my soul's secrets and the mystical knowledge to help suffering humanity in its search for inner peace.

Before my birth, higher powers decreed that I must live a worldly existence this time, a time of final spiritual testing, for it is nearly impossible to be non-physical in a physical world.

Suddenly, the secret universe opens its spiritual gates for me and I find what I've been searching for. I discover a cosmic El Dorado, overflowing with wealth beyond humanity's wildest dreams and most extravagant imaginings. Virgin worlds and new galaxies, all are visible now and vibrate with a living light.

As I'm guided further through vast invisible dimensions by angels, *my ethereal body is changing. Suddenly, I am spirit. I know myself as "the real I," the creator of karma, the breather of every breath and the thinker of every thought. Pure spirit slips out of its earthly form and becomes an airy mist.*

My essence floats, weightless.

My spiritual form changes again into a delicate vapor of luminous colors and I am wrapped in ultimate love, surrounded by the wondrous living light. Like a luxurious magic carpet, the profound light carries me to lofty celestial heights and glorious inner dimensions.

The heartbeat of the universe pulsates with a new "music" I had never heard before. *The Symphony of Creation.*

Space and time do not exist here, nor is there any need for their existence, for in this divine sphere, it is always NOW. Inner mysteries and rites of passage urge my spirit to progress further and not to fear.

"Be not afraid, little one," my luminous guide tells me.

Suddenly, an inner burst of consciousness transforms me, transcending all thought. I am a new being made of an ethereal living light. I float and drift in the purest love that is the cradle of Creation, a shimmering cosmic ocean of pure spirit that welcomes me to its sacred sanctuary. *This is the moment I've waited for, all of my lives.* The fountain of eternal youth is mine for the asking, along with total enlightenment as past-life awareness is raised to spectacular new heights.

In an instant, I experience the final ecstasy, a total oneness with Creation itself, an ultimate bliss which challenges adequate description in any of earth's languages.

On that sublime journey where all dreams lead, I finally discover the fate of our earth, the life-span of this universe and the real reason for our existence.

Destiny and hard-earned karma over the centuries have brought me to this sublime night of my second initiation, a cosmic dawn of consciousness, a torrent of revelations and a total oneness with the birth of the universe, while back in the forest's glade, Lance's loving spirit protects my physical body while "I" am not there.

"The real I" is still in vast spiritual regions, searching the mystical corridors of time.

I now see (and understand) the reasons for everything that has happened to me, good or bad. Until this night, memories of, *and reasons for*, my past lives had always been vague images with only a few details and some former names.

Now, *the cause of everything* is clear. Welcome details bring further enlightenment and I learn more about the hidden universe than I ever thought possible.

In *FOREVER*, the revelations come gently this time.

I am shown why the Creator has isolated me for several years in an interstate move I hadn't wanted and fought against because it removed me from the center of all my interests, as well as the exciting city of my birth, the source of my spiritual abilities and the scene of my first initiation.

Yet, it was in the countryside, with its vast woodland views, that I found time to enjoy the quiet serenity of nature and the calm contemplation of universal truths.

I thought that this interstate move was a curse, but it proved to be a blessing, a golden mask obscured.

The universe had prepared me well for this night. Lance's voice, Richard's music, each had been a golden bridge of stars across the vast universe, a bridge that ultimately led me to this wondrous spiritual region. With their loving help, I've turned the key in the lock on the sacred door to *FOREVER*, the paradise which existed before the first faint beginnings of time and will continue to exist past the end of our space-time universe as we know it. I'm eternally indebted to both of them.

Everything is so clear now. People we've known, loved and hated in our past lives are here with us, in brand-new lives with new names, new identities and new roles to play in this grand drama. Each life links with all others, bonded by love or hate. Whether you call it fate, destiny or karma, the cosmic law of cause-and-effect is clear. What we do to others will come back to haunt us or bless us, and random acts of kindness or cruelty will always return to us. We're not punished *for* our past mistakes. We're taught *by* them, by having to *live* them. Rebirth is merely a guideline to balance the cosmic scales of justice as each hour, we choose our directions, designing the exact futures we deserve through our thoughts and actions now. For many of us, no other principle can explain the mysteries of our lives with such supreme logic, exquisite accuracy and perfect justice.

But the greatest secret I've learned is this: *We're all in the act of becoming what we've always been. PERFECT.* When this is accomplished, suffering humanity will finally cast off its dense physical bodies, take a giant leap and become divine.

Floating in deep contemplation of all I'd just learned, I felt myself slipping back into the physical world, being pulled away from *FOREVER* and back toward my waiting body.

I don't want to leave . . .

But my profound desire to stay had been subdued *for me*. The silver cord, my physical body's lifeline, shimmered brightly in the reflected glow of *FOREVER*, where I'd learned life's greatest secrets.

Pulsating with a luminous light, my silver cord became shorter and shorter as it pulled me back to my physical body.

Suddenly, I had an oppressive sense of time, of past-present-future, of birth and death, of pain and sorrow.

The earth seemed dark and dismal in my sight.

I desperately wanted to go back there, back to peace and happiness and love . . .

To the realm of living light, where it is always NOW.

An epic sunrise, full of fire and romance, covered the earth with a warm extravagance as my spirit relaxed into my physical form as effortlessly as a hand slipping into a silk-lined leather glove.

My consciousness fully returned to the physical world.

I was once again in my feminine body, the living temple of life, spirit, enlightenment and love.

Slowly, I opened my eyes.

During the night, snow had fallen.

A luminous frost blanketed the ground with a sparkling white cloak.

My skin should have been icy-cold, wearing only a sheer nightgown for all those nighttime hours, but surprisingly, my flesh was warm as a summer day.

All these hours, Lance had patiently awaited my return, protecting me from danger and from the relentless cold.

A serene heat radiated from my body, visible as curving waves of pulsating golden light.

A second energy-force had wrapped itself around me, warming me with love's radiant colors.

It was Lance, warming me with his own power and love.

His luminous spirit surrounded me with a golden cocoon of warmth as we moved up the pathway, past the tall evergreen trees, out of December's forest and onto the rear lawn leading to my countryside home.

Frosty snow crunched beneath my satin slippers with each step, but Lance made no sound as he drifted beside me. Together, we wandered into the home filled with love and the sound of our son's music.

The world had not yet awakened . . .

Chapter 18:

THE DAY AFTER FOREVER

In a world where centuries may be a mere flicker in time, the words *life expectancy* suddenly take on an exciting new meaning. Through the mirror of our current lives, we can finally know the *why* of everything, and because my awakening has answered so many puzzling aspects of my current life, the facts may help to explain the mystifying events in your own life, especially the true origins of your close relationships.

The following stands as a living, breathing example of how our past lives can affect our current existence and will show you how the Elizabeth-lifetime has touched me so very intimately, in ways I hadn't suspected until my inner journey.

I've never been able to stand the sight of blood.

I never wear the color red.

Now I know why.

Every year in this lifetime, I've dreaded the coming of summer and I always avoid seeing dramas that portray pioneer massacres. *Anyone who knows me can verify this.*

I've always been drawn to exquisite music, the theater, the performing arts and all forms of dance, especially ballet.

I've always preferred dark-haired romantic gentlemen with elegance and a dramatic flair, men who look like Lance.

Memories of him? *Absolutely.*

Lance and I have an extensive past history, with shared lives lived in idyllic places . . . .

ANCIENT EGYPT: He was the Pharaoh and I was the daughter who made the ultimate sacrifice for him; *ANCIENT PERSIA:* As a very young girl, I was captured in a raid on my village and made a slave. He was the ruling Sultan who saved my life; and *MEDIEVAL ENGLAND,* an era of chivalry, falconry and knighthood, where he was my devoted brother. Someday, I'll reveal devastating secrets about these past lives, but for now, see how easily the past fits into the present as we search this dress-rehearsal we call *life* for our answers.

My former husband, Lance: *How I wish I could tell you his true name, but I cannot violate his privacy, especially now.* Ethan, my brother, *is now my favorite friend.*

Kirsten Holm, the gentle midwife: *my father's mother. A warm, bountiful woman and the mother of several sons, she was nearly blind and generous to a fault.* My mother and father then, *my loving parents again.* The native woman who tried to warn me about the coming massacre: *a trusted friend.* All the pioneers I knew then, *good friends now.* Pastor Wesley: *minister of the church where I spent my earliest years. He was reluctantly assigned to another church thousands of miles away, and when he left, his life and his warmth went with him.*

The children born of Elizabeth and Lance, the children of the frontier, are listed here in the order of their birth.

<u>Richard</u> (Lion-heart) *is now on the inner spiritual planes composing extraordinary new music while he patiently waits for a suitable birth, along with* <u>Logan Halliday</u>, *who is also hoping for a modern-day incarnation.*

<u>Purity</u>: *my mother's mother and an extraordinary woman, a prime example of deep faith and supreme goodness.* <u>Anne</u>: *a sweet friend.* <u>Charles & James</u>, *reborn as twin boys.*

Each of these reunions was happy, except for *<u>the Leader</u>.* You'd be too shocked if I told you who he was, as well as the sinister and murderous way he entered my life. History has not given him the fame he wanted and his name is unknown in the history of his own people. Born a white male in our present time, he was still brutal, vicious and intimidating. He made it very clear that he desired me, but there was no rape in this life.

And this time, the death was his own.

Although all of my deepest spiritual questions have been thoroughly answered by rebirth and its eternal handmaiden, karma,* you don't have to believe in reincarnation to take pleasure from Elizabeth's passionate long-ago adventure, and from Lance, the vital actor who journeyed here so long ago to keep an appointment with a sweet love and a cruel destiny.

---

* *Fate; Destiny; The cosmic principle of individual rewards and disciplines in this life or previous lives.*

When I speak about the tragedies of pioneer life, I speak with the tearstained voice of one who was there. You can imagine how painful it was for me to speak of our massacre and the tortures that preceded it, but I've always been dedicated to the truth, and some truths are not pretty. The truth must never be altered *for any reason* and the facts will always speak for themselves. Some people might prefer that I had chosen to "overlook" that day of death and terror here in these pages, but the choice was never mine, because *it really happened.* Three adults and six children (1 unborn) died on that day. This was, *and is,* part of our tragic story, and as such, it belongs here.

My memories ended on the day I died. Therefore, I can only speak of things I personally knew, witnessed and endured. Yet, I do not hate any of the men who murdered us.

As for Lance and I, our lyrical duo has become a solo performance for me now. Memories of him are sharp and clear. They come to me in a heartbeat, surfacing during my days and disrupting my sleep in the dark hours of night. But when I see him performing, time melts away, the pain is gone and we're together again, not thousands of miles and an ocean apart.

Still, the sad evidence is there for us to see. Some of his performances were completed several years ago. More recent ones reveal declining power and disappearing strength. These, and other subtle visible clues are easily detected through the eyes of love. In a recent photo, his eyes reveal an anguished sorrow, telling the world that tragedy has entered his life.

Sometimes, friends see the same look in my eyes.

It's true that tormented emotions have taken their toll on me emotionally, but when I feel his presence I am comforted, for he surrounds me with his love.

Whenever I close my eyes, he is there.

A widow's grief reaches out to me across the centuries and I mourn for a man who died nearly two centuries ago. His voice, with its seductive rhythm, guides me now. The slow and sweet vibrato of its velvet touch soothes me, and the devouring intimacy of his phantom kiss lingers long in my consciousness.

Although we are torn apart by a tragic misconnection, our love remains alive, like two candle-flames in a darkened sanctuary, each light glowing brighter whenever it touches the other in a celestial embrace.

Our saga is truly a mystery within a mystery, within yet *another* mystery, a challenge worthy of the world's finest sleuth or the wisdom of King Solomon himself.

But we're lost in a storm.

I cannot accept the most recent revelations about the true state of his health, for I *know* the serious nature of his tragic illness, one that is kept secret from all except those who are closest to him. If only I could touch him and heal him, he might live . . . I hope he hurries. Time is short for him.

I will not ask why he is always so near.

I'm afraid of the answer.

I may never again know Lance's touch or the warmth of his breath on my face, but if destiny reunites us before this lifetime ends, then we'll gaze into each other's eyes and find our love, waiting there. He will call me "Elizabeth, my lady," unasked, for our love has a deep and a passionate history.

Perhaps this book will guide him here. Someone may give it to him as a gift or he might see it in a bookstore window. A compelling fascination will draw him to it and he'll take it home with him.

He may be reading these words at this very moment.

Or perhaps he'll be visiting someone and notice this book on a coffee table. Some invisible force will urge him to open it and he'll reach out with those large expressive hands of his. As he holds this book, a lightning-touch will compel him to look inside, and he'll open it to a page he is destined to see.

Our star-crossed love will awaken him with its secret mysteries and its intimate memories. The facts will strike a sweetly familiar chord, the endless love will rise within him again, his conscious mind will remember and he'll follow his heart here, to the ethereal woman who was known in the far distant past as Elizabeth.

Elizabeth . . . his cosmic birthright.

The author of this book.

Perhaps he already remembers, and is on his way.

NOT .... The End

AFTERGLOW

A Special Message for you, the reader

As your gentle guide, I've stripped my soul bare for you in these pages, escorting you on a true and secret journey into the distant past, an innocent era when one of America's most daring adventures occurred. You felt a virgin's passion awaken when I first saw "Lance," the man who became my husband.

You lived our long journey and our dangerous adventures on the pioneer trail, you were there *with us* on the day we found our sanctuary, and in your mind's eye, you witnessed the horrors that destiny demanded of us all, even the children and the unborn, on the bloodstained day I call *firestorm*.

Then, just like a passenger on a starship headed for undiscovered galaxies, you drifted on cosmic currents into our present time. It was *here* that the first modern-day miracle happened, the night I saw Lance's face. And it was here that I heard my former son's music, a sonic landscape that unlocked the doorway to all the amazing inner dimensions of our world.

Then, we time-shifted into a region without time.

You soared freely beyond our space-time universe into vast invisible dimensions. You also discovered angelic beings made of light and the one Creator all religions share.

The future is all around you and the distant past is only a breath away from remembrance. All you need is the desire.

When you remember who and what you really are, when you can feel the potential divinity glowing within you, you'll stand taller, you'll walk more confidently and you'll look to the source of your life for the truth.

Higher talents will develop.

Second sight.

Sixth sense.

Your life can change in a heartbeat.

You are a far more magnificent being than you realize.

If you decide to follow the path to conscious immortality, you'll discover that it leads you deeper into yourself, so cross the threshold of your doubts and enter the great silence.

Seek the perfection that is already within you and your consciousness will exist and flourish where eagles soar.

A new confidence, *an inner knowing*, will emerge when you give yourself permission to advance past the limits of our physical world and explore the beauty of inner space.

Magical worlds await you.

I wish you a bountiful and wondrous journey.

Go with an open mind and a searching heart as you discover what it's like to live and move in the higher realms of our existence, where all things are possible.

Confound time itself as you unlock the miracles that dark centuries have hidden from you.

Demand your destiny.

Reach for the stars.

Empower your life.

Always trust your own instincts.

You'll find your miracle.

You'll find your place of *inner peace.*

Listen to the voice within you, for that majestic sound is the life-force that sustains each breath you take and which nurtures this vast universe, as well as all the other yet-unknown worlds beyond.

Remain as receptive as a chalice, and the gifts will come.

Above all, be happy . . .

My love goes with you, each step of the way.

Your gentle guide, Elizabeth

This book would not be complete if I omitted *a special tribute*
to the man with whom I shared my love and life in the distant past.

EAST OF REMEMBRANCE, WEST OF SORROW

It seems like only yesterday, you and I built fairytale castles in the sand and rode carousel horses on the solar-wind. Romantic images linger, like afterglow, a mercurial montage of misty harbor lights and softest eider-down. I remember . . . oh, how clearly I remember . . . fiery sunsets and windstorm passions, memorable champagne and cream-colored silk, my curvaceous body melting into yours with a Lorelei's siren call.

The twilight of our lives together has vanished, and in its place, nightfall and starlight and a dream denied. Yet, only moments ago, your star-filled voice called to me again with its passion and its plaintive longing, only a heartbeat away.

In my journal, I write words for you alone, then whisper aloud, "Good night, sweet prince," believing that you are gone from me. But you are not, and you make your presence known to me with your usual Shakespearean flair. . .

"I beg you, my lady, do not beseech me to say good night."

Your soul cries out to me in agony as you desperately try to achieve the impossible, trying to penetrate the luminous barrier between us. The air around me quivers and trembles with your heroic effort, your noble suffering.

My cries echo on the still night air.

*"No! Please stop! I cannot bear to witness your torment,"
I cry as I shut my eyes, but still you are there, struggling with a
knight's valor. I scream out your true name, but you continue to
endure your torture with a hero's courage. Finally, you pierce
the silvery veil between us with nothing but the power of your
love. Suddenly, you're here! Your phantom embrace surrounds
me with your love and finds me willing.*

*You whisper to me, words of the idyllic beauty that was
ours for such a brief moment in time. You whisper into my hair,
profound secrets and veiled mysteries known only by us.*

*It is as I've suspected, my love. You have read every word
of this, standing behind me, invisible and eternal, my beloved
muse. You speak in a whisper, I listen with my heart . . . .*

*My heart soars like the North wind, for I understand
what you are trying to say. You will continue to point the way
in which I must go, and all the while, I will be surrounded by
your love and shielded from all harm.*

*Then you whisper words so sweet, so enchanting to hear,
these eternal words . . . .*

"You are my life after life, my very last celestial breath."

*I close my eyes, I breathe you in and I am filled with
your essence. We will never be apart again, my love, for you are
a part of me now.*

I wanted tomorrow . . . .
   You gave me yesterday . . . .
      Together, we will demand forever.

Eternally, Elizabeth

ABOUT THE AUTHOR

A.E.Witte's multi-media artistry is strictly prime-time. This popular writer's extensive literary credits include top-rated television networks in New York and California, the creative environment of Madison Avenue advertising, and many prestigious publications read world-wide.

This award-winning writer and metaphysical explorer always brings a consistent professionalism and extraordinary insight to the phenomena of past-life awareness, and because of a dazzling expertise and extensive first-hand knowledge, A.E.Witte is eminently qualified to chronicle the paranormal events you've found in *PASSION, POWER & PROPHECY*. Along the way, the veiled parts of our existence are unveiled in this compelling page-turner, a landmark literary work as contemporary as today and as promising as tomorrow. *Please note: At A.E.Witte's request, all mail addressed to this author is first opened and carefully examined by our Security Officers, then forwarded on.*

The author is currently living in Hawaii.

STATUS PUBLISHERS, INC.

220

LIBRARY OF CONGRESS

CATALOGING-IN-PUBLICATION DATA

Witte, A. E., date.
      Passion, power and prophecy :
      based on actual events /
      by A. E. Witte. -- 1st ed.
          p.   cm.
      Includes index.
      ISBN 1-888122-00-5
      1. Spiritual life -- Miscellanea.
      2. Reincarnation -- Miscellanea.
   I. Title.
   BF1999.W64   1996
   133.9'01'3092--dc20
   [B]   95-25582
                                  CIP

INDEX

INDEX

INDEX

I N D E X